THE STUDENT AID GAME

MEETING NEED AND REWARDING TALENT IN AMERICAN HIGHER EDUCATION

Michael S. McPherson
and Morton Owen Schapiro

PRINCETON UNIVERSITY PRESS   PRINCETON, NEW JERSEY

Library of Congress Cataloging-in-Publication Data
McPherson, Michael S.
  The student aid game : meeting need and rewarding talent in
American higher education / Michael S. McPherson and Morton Owen
Schapiro.
      p.   cm.
  Includes bibliographical references and index.
  ISBN 0-691-05783-4 (cloth : alk. paper)
  1. Student aid—United States.   2. College students—Scholarships,
fellowships, etc.—United States.   3. Education, Higher—United
States—Finance.   I. Schapiro, Morton Owen.   II. Title.
LB2337.4.M32   1998
378.3'0973—dc21   97-14999

Publication of this book has been aided by a grant from
the Andrew W. Mellon Foundation

This book has been composed in Palatino

Princeton University Press books are printed on acid-free paper
and meet the guidelines for permanence and durability of the
Committee on Production Guidelines for Book Longevity of the
Council on Library Resources

http://pup.princeton.edu

Printed in the United States of America

10 9 8 7 6 5 4 3

We dedicate this book to our children,
Sean and Steven McPherson and
Alissa and Matt Schapiro,
who have done such a fine job of
making us aware of both their talents
and their needs

Contents

Figures and Tables   vii

Foreword by William G. Bowen and Harold T. Shapiro   ix

Acknowledgments   xiii

PART ONE: INTRODUCTION   1

**1. Meeting Need and Rewarding Talent: Student Aid
in the U.S. System of Higher Education Finance**   5

**2. Changing the Rules: The New Strategic Role of Student
Aid**   15

PART TWO: STUDENT AID AND EDUCATIONAL
OPPORTUNITY: ARE WE KEEPING COLLEGE
AFFORDABLE?   23

3. Prices and Aid: The Growing Burden on Families   25

**4. Access: Student Response to Higher Prices—and Higher
Returns**   37

5. Choice: How Ability to Pay Affects College Options   42

6. The Future of College Affordability   49

PART THREE: STUDENT AID AND INSTITUTIONAL
STRATEGY   53

7. Student Aid in Institutional Finance   55

8. How Government Aid Shapes Colleges' Behavior   81

9. Student Aid as a Competitive Weapon   91

PART FOUR: THE SPECIAL CASE OF MERIT AID   105

10. Merit Aid: Its Place in History and Its Role in Society   107

11. The Institutional Perspective   116

12. The Student Perspective   122

13. Conclusion: Merit Aid—Good or Bad?   130

PART FIVE: THE FUTURE OF STUDENT AID   133

14. Where Do We Go from Here?   135

Notes   145

Bibliography   153

Index   157

Figures and Tables

Figures

Figure 3.1. Financing of Undergraduate Tuition at Private Nonprofit Institutions, 1986–87 and 1992–93.   33

Figure 3.2. Financing of Undergraduate Tuition at Public Institutions, 1986–87 and 1992–93.   34

Figure 3.3. Financing of Undergraduate Tuition at Private For-Profit Institutions, 1986–87 and 1992–93.   36

Tables

Table 3.1. Shares of Educational and General Revenue, Public and Private Institutions, Selected Academic Years, 1939–1993 (%).   26

Table 3.2. Shares of Higher Education Revenue, by Source, Selected Academic Years, 1939–1993 (%).   27

Table 3.3. Aid Awarded to Students, by Source, Selected Academic Years, 1963–1995 (millions of dollars).   28

Table 3.4. Distribution of Pell Grant Funds to Independent Students and Proprietary Schools, Selected Academic Years, 1973–1994 (%).   31

Table 3.5. Financing of Undergraduate Tuitions, 1986–87 and 1992–93 (in 1992–93 dollars).   32

Table 4.1. College Enrollment Rates of High School Graduates (%).   38

Table 5.1. Freshman Enrollment, by Income Background, across Institution Types (%).   44

Table 7.1. Expenditures at Research and Doctoral Universities (Carnegie Research I and II, Doctoral I and II), 1987–1994 (in 1993–94 dollars).   57

Table 7.2. Revenues of Research and Doctoral Universities (Carnegie Research I and II, Doctoral I and II), 1987–1994 (in 1993–94 dollars).   61

Table 7.3. Expenditures at Comprehensive Universities (Carnegie Comprehensive I and II), 1987–1994 (in 1993–94) dollars.   64

Table 7.4. Revenues of Comprehensive Universities (Carnegie Comprehensive I and II), 1987–1994 (in 1993–94 dollars).   66

Table 7.5.   Expenditures at Liberal Arts Colleges (Carnegie
             Liberal Arts I and II), 1987–1994 (in 1993–94
             dollars).   69
Table 7.6.   Revenues of Liberal Arts Colleges (Carnegie
             Liberal Arts I and II), 1987–1994 (in 1993–94
             dollars).   71
Table 7.7.   Expenditures at Community Colleges (Public
             Carnegie Two-Year Schools), 1987–1994 (in
             1993–94 dollars).   73
Table 7.8.   Revenues at Community Colleges (Public Carnegie
             Two-Year Schools, 1987–1994 (in 1993–94 dollars).   73
Table 7.9.   Breakdown of Expenditures, 1987 and 1994 (%).   74
Table 7.10. Breakdown of Revenues, 1987 and 1994 (%).   75
Table 9.1.   Admissions Profile, Conjectural University.   92
Table 9.2.   Revised Admissions Policy, Conjectural University.   95
Table 11.1. Non-Need Aid per Freshman, by Institution Type
             and Carnegie Classification, 1983–84 and 1991–92.   117
Table 11.2. Non-Need Aid per Freshman, by Admissions
             Difficulty, 1983–84 and 1991–92.   119
Table 12.1. Public and Private Four-Year Institutional
             Non-Need Awards, 1990.   123
Table 12.2. Private Four-Year Institutional Non-Need Awards,
             1990.   124
Table 12.3. Public Four-Year Institutional Non-Need Awards,
             1990.   125

Foreword _____

WILLIAM G. BOWEN AND HAROLD T. SHAPIRO

SINCE THE FOUNDING of the earliest colleges, student aid has provided educational opportunities for a certain number of students who are, in the ancient lexicon, "needy and deserving," and providing full access to such students has been a long-sought goal of financial aid programs. How well these programs serve that purpose today is one of the central questions examined by McPherson and Schapiro in this timely book. In addition, they investigate carefully the relatively recent tendency for student aid to be used by many colleges and universities for "strategic" purposes—as a sophisticated tool designed to help the institution attract enough students of the requisite quality. The growing use of merit aid, and the increasing prevalence of discounting, are practices that have major implications for students and families seeking to finance a college education. These private-sector decisions have been made in the context of continuing changes in governmental student aid policies and even broader trends in public support for higher education (with larger and larger shares of the cost of higher education being borne by individuals and their families); after describing these developments, McPherson and Schapiro assess how effectively Pell grants, loan programs, and newly proposed tax incentives can be expected to serve the needs of society.

This is a highly complex territory, with interactions of all kinds going on, and one of the real contributions made by McPherson and Schapiro is their emphasis on the need to think through carefully how colleges and universities will respond to various federal initiatives. They are right in maintaining that we need a much better theoretical understanding or guiding model of the behavior of non-profit institutions—otherwise, we may not recognize under what circumstances new tax incentives, for example, are likely to reduce student aid outlays by colleges and universities. As an example of the dangers of proceeding without such guidance, Secretary Bennett is shown to have based his assertion that increased Pell grants would serve mainly to stimulate tuition increases on a quite mistaken model of institutional behavior (or on no model at all).

Behavioral responses of students and their families are also studied in detail, and one of the important conclusions is that changes in the net cost of going to college have had very little effect on enrollment rates of students from high-income families—but considerable effect on enrollment rates of students from lower-income families. McPherson and Schapiro document how rising costs (net of increases in financial aid) during the last decades have caused the gap in enrollment rates between the higher- and lower-income students to grow, as well as the gap in enrollment rates between whites and blacks (which has widened from about 5 percentage points in the late 70s to 12 percentage points in the early 90s).

As the authors note "These facts make the trend of the past few years to reduce real funding of Pell grants and increase funding for loans all the more unsettling" (p. 41). There is, after all, strong evidence that federal grant dollars are effectively targeted on low-income students and do encourage enrollment, whereas loan funds do not appear to affect many decisions to go to college. McPherson and Schapiro are also critical of the Clinton plan to provide various tax incentives, since they believe that much of the tax revenue foregone will be "absorbed" by institutions and individuals without much effect on enrollment patterns. They recognize, however, that political realities have to be faced, and especially the apparently strong preference of the American people for tax reductions rather than improvements in spending programs such as those that might fund the Pell grant program.

Over at least the last three decades, student aid policies in America have been concerned not only with access (can a student go to college at all) but also with choice (what kind of college can the student attend). A detailed inspection of recently available data on trends in the types of schools attended by students from different income groups yields a number of findings. One that will surprise many people is that, contrary to much popular lore, there does *not* appear to have been a "middle-income melt" from private colleges or private universities. Rather, there has been an "upper-income melt" from private four-year colleges—a finding that helps us understand the fiscal problems of many of these colleges and their aggressive marketing and price-discounting. Many of the most affluent students now attend universities, both private and public: 47% of the first-time freshmen from the highest income category enrolled at a university in 1994, as compared with 39% in 1980. Conversely, the fraction of students from the lowest income category attending public two-year colleges has continued to increase; nearly half of all the first-time freshman from this income category entered community colleges in 1994; less than 10% of students from the highest-income category made the same enrollment decision. These patterns and trends are attributed, in large part, to a combination of rising college costs and the failure of student aid to keep pace.

Both authors of this study, well-known as economists and long-time students of financial aid, now occupy senior administrative positions—McPherson as president of Macalester College and Schapiro as Dean of the College of Letters, Arts and Sciences at the University of Southern California. This blend of training and experience serves them particularly well when they discuss the sometimes controversial subject of merit aid. They resolutely refuse to be moralistic on the subject, noting (correctly, we believe) that it is easy to be in favor of strictly need-based aid if you represent a prestigious institution that has very large numbers of well-qualified applicants, many of whom come from affluent families. If, on the other hand, you represent a liberal arts college that is struggling to meet enrollment targets and that needs to attract a certain number of top students each year to retain its standing, you are much more likely to be in favor of some form of merit aid. As a student of public policy once put it "Where you stand depends on where you sit." College administrators and trustees alike will find useful the detailed outline of alternative approaches to student aid, and ways of judging trade-offs, provided by McPherson and Schapiro.[1]

At the same time that they respect institutional perspectives, the authors are also acutely conscious of the issues of social policy that underlie this debate. A long (and very interesting) discussion of the social impact of merit aid leads to the conclusion that the concentration of merit aid at the less selective institutions may serve a useful role by spreading high-talent students among a broader mix of schools; nevertheless, the resources foregone by providing merit aid are growing, and this has to be worrisome from the standpoint of the colleges and universities.

In considering all of these issues, and others, McPherson and Schapiro are careful to marshal the relevant empirical evidence (assembling, in the process, a rich set of materials that will be of interest in their own right to students of higher education), to subject the data to questioning borne of a well-specified analytical framework, and to focus attention on the policy issues that are of paramount importance. Those of us who believe that higher education must continue to be a powerful engine of opportunity in our society will find this study highly informative. We will also find that it raises troubling questions about our continuing ability to "meet need and reward talent" in the most efficacious way.

---

[1] Readers of this volume may also be interested in a detailed study by Elizabeth A. Duffy and Idana Goldberg of trends in admission and financial aid at liberal arts colleges in Massachusetts and Ohio, *Crafting a Class*, that will be published by Princeton University Press this fall.

Acknowledgments _____

OUR GREATEST debt is to Bill Bowen of the Mellon Foundation. His intellectual leadership, firm confidence in the worth of this project, and sage advice throughout our work have proved invaluable. Our colleagues in the Williams Project on the Economics of Higher Education, most notably Gordon Winston and Henry Bruton, have been a continuing source of insight as well as thoughtful criticism. Thanks as well to Ron Ehrenberg, whose comments have helped us improve our work. Larry Litten offered very helpful advice on our work on merit aid, and Phil Wick was very generous in sharing with us a draft of his study of the history of merit aid, on which we have drawn in part in Chapter 10. Ethan Lewis, Ivan Yen, and Anne Karabinos provided exceptionally capable research assistance.

We acknowledge the support of the Andrew W. Mellon Foundation for the research underlying this book. We are also very grateful for the support of the Finance Center of the Consortium for Policy Research in Education, funded by the U.S. Department of Education's Office of Educational Research (Cooperative Agreement No. R117G10039-91) and the National Center for Postsecondary Improvement (Agreement No. R309A60001). Allan Odden, who oversaw our work for the Finance Center, was enormously helpful throughout. Parts of the book were presented at seminars at Princeton University, the National Bureau of Economic Research, Williams College, the Stanford Forum on Higher Education Futures, and the U.S. Department of Education. We are grateful to all these groups for their attention and comments.

Part One

INTRODUCTION

STUDENT AID is much in the news today, and much of that news is unsettling. Just a few years ago, the Justice Department was investigating some of the most prestigious colleges and universities in the country for allegedly conspiring to fix prices by coordinating their financial aid offers. More recently, we have read about universities that use sophisticated computer programs to identify students who passionately want to enroll so that they can exploit their eagerness by offering them smaller financial aid packages (Stecklow 1996) and others who proclaim their commitment to awarding financial aid only on the basis of need while at the same time offering their best admissions candidates guaranteed summer jobs and research stipends (Shea 1996). Meanwhile, there is growing evidence that the resources available to give the lowest-income college students a meaningful choice among educational alternatives are dwindling and there is widespread worry that governments, both state and federal, will continue to back away from their commitments to support the education of needy students through grants and loans.

If we step back from the headlines, it is clear that several basic forces are imposing rapid change on the role and operation of financial aid in the U.S. higher education system. First, the persistent gap between the level of governmental services Americans want and the level of taxation they are willing to endure to support those services has produced relentless budgetary pressure at both state and federal levels. Higher education programs remain popular, but year by year the competition between them and other high-priority uses of funds for matters like health care and prisons grows more fierce. Second, individual colleges and universities, beset by their own fiscal problems and by intense competition for highly qualified, fee-paying students, have ceased to think of their financial aid efforts principally as a noble charitable opportunity and have instead come to focus on the financial aid operation as a key strategic weapon both in recruiting students and in maximizing institutional revenues. Finally, parents and students, increasingly worried about their ability to pay for college and increasingly persuaded that a college education provides the only hope of a secure economic future, are focused on getting the best possible education at the lowest possible price.

Where, in this highly conflictual and fluid setting, does the public interest lie? For the past thirty years, the national agenda in higher education has been defined by the goals of "access" and "choice," access labeling the goal of ensuring that no American is denied the opportunity to attend some kind of postsecondary institution by reason of inability to pay and choice labeling the goal of giving students a reasonable menu of alternative colleges from which they can pick the one that best fits their needs. The provision of public higher education by state governments, with hefty institutional subsidies that aim to keep costs to students and parents low, has been for many years the principal public vehicle for attaining these goals. The conception of the state government as the source of a fully articulated range of low-cost educational options perhaps reached its apotheosis with the publication of California's influential Master Plan in 1960, which laid out a scheme for a three-tiered system of community colleges, state colleges, and University of California campuses, within which every California high school graduate could find a suitable place. The federal commitment to these goals has roots in the post–World War II GI Bill but became settled national policy under the leadership first of Lyndon Johnson and then of Richard Nixon. Private colleges and universities themselves signed on to these broad principles through the development in the 1950s of formal "needs analysis" systems aimed at scientific measurement of families' ability to pay for college and through the adoption, with varying degrees of sincerity, of the principles that only students with demonstrated need should receive financial aid and that all the needy students a college accepted should receive as much aid as they needed.

Although these principles have never been fully realized in practice, it is clear that the pressures to move away from them, at the state, federal, and institutional levels, are stronger than ever. The question of whether the choices made by individual governments, institutions, and families add up to a result that makes sense from a systemwide standpoint is increasingly urgent. Our aim in this book is to address that large question by looking at the system and its parts: by examining at the system level how the higher education financing system has evolved in recent decades, and with what consequences for "access" and "choice," and by considering at the level of the actors in the system—states, institutions, and students—how their strategic choices have shaped the outcomes that we see. The result, we believe, is an analysis that will allow us to see more clearly how far we have come and thereby permit us to think more realistically about options for the future.

In this introductory part of the volume, we provide in Chapter 1 an overview of the role student aid has played in the past and plays now in American higher education finance and in Chapter 2 a broad sketch of how the shifting environment of higher education is changing the way colleges and universities themselves approach the student aid "game."

Part Two of the book looks in some depth at how undergraduate education is financed in the United States, examining differences for various sectors and for students of differing family backgrounds. We review the implications of recent financing trends for access to and choice of undergraduate college and then step back to gauge the implications of these national trends for the future of college opportunity.

Part Three moves the focus from broad national trends to the workings of institutions. We first look in detail at how various categories of colleges and universities have been changing in their financing patterns—both their sources of revenue and their patterns of expenditure. This leads us to the important question of how colleges' financing decisions may be influenced by changes in external incentives, such as those created by government programs. A program of federal student aid or of tax cuts for college tuition, for example, might have its impact either offset or reinforced by the impact the program has on how colleges use their own aid funds. This set of issues is, we think, particularly salient for the president's proposed new tax program. We argue in Part Three and further in Chapter 14 that the proposed tax cuts threaten to yield a plethora of unintended consequences. Finally in Part Three, we zero in on the strategic competitive choices made by institutions in their pricing and aid decisions. This strategic dimension is increasingly important in understanding the higher education system and for thinking intelligently about policy options.

Many colleges are concerned with the strategic choice of getting involved with no-need or merit aid, and this fascinating phenomenon comes in for sustained attention in Part Four. We consider the attractions and pitfalls of merit aid from the viewpoint of both students and institutions, and we consider the question of whether and when merit aid policies may serve the broad public interest.

Our conclusions in Part Five focus on the implications of our findings for policy at the government level and for individual schools. The federal government has only limited leverage over this large and highly decentralized system, and nothing is more important than that it use the resources it has with intelligence and forethought to achieve major social goals. It is our sense that both federal and state governments have fallen short on their responsibilities, and we try to say why we think so and how they could do better. Individual colleges and universities face policy choices too, and these choices have a civic aspect to them. While resisting the temptation to preach to leaders who face limited options in a highly competitive environment, we offer some broad principles that may provide some guidance.

1

Meeting Need and Rewarding Talent

STUDENT AID IN THE U.S. SYSTEM
OF HIGHER EDUCATION FINANCE

THIS CHAPTER provides an overview of the evolution of the role of student aid in American higher education and a brief review of how undergraduate education in the United States is currently financed. The evolution of student aid has been shaped over the past four decades by a powerful governing vision of a pricing-plus-aid system that would eliminate ability to pay for college as a factor in college choice. Although that vision has never come close to realization, we will see in this chapter and the next that it has had an important role in shaping the programs, both government and institutional, that currently exist.

Evolution of the Student Aid Vision

Scholarship awards to "needy and deserving" students have been a feature of American higher education from its earliest days. The phrase "needy and deserving" suggests the dual purposes that such grants in aid to college students have always aimed to achieve. On one hand, there is the desire to recognize and reward highly meritorious students and thereby encourage them to invest more in their education. The aim of encouraging the further education of more successful and promising students may be seen as intrinsically worthy, if educational merit is valued for its own sake, but it also has the more pragmatic purpose of allowing society to benefit through the development of the talents of the most able students. On the other hand, there is the desire to extend the benefits of higher education more widely by helping young adults in financial need to attain more education. Extending educational benefits to the less advantaged may be valued intrinsically in terms of contributing to equal opportunity and fairness, but again there is a pragmatic justification in terms of society's interest in seeing that the talents of the less advantaged do not go to waste.

These two objectives are plainly partly supportive and partly conflicting. From a practical standpoint, the more affluent among highly talented youth are less likely to need the stimulus of scholarship awards to be encouraged to continue their education, and social recognition of their talents can be achieved in significant measure without spending money. So even from the standpoint of rewarding talent, there is a case for focusing scholarship resources on needy students. And from the standpoint of equal opportunity, there is little point to devoting scholarship funds to students whose aptitudes and inclinations make them unlikely to benefit from higher education; such folks may deserve social support on grounds of equity, but not in the form of financial assistance in going to college. Yet although this suggests a broad overlap between the policies that would be favored on grounds of rewarding merit and on grounds of meeting need, there is plainly a lot of room for difference in emphasis and interpretation as schools and society work out policies for financial aid.

Until the 1950s, the policies schools adopted in awarding scholarships were largely uncoordinated and idiosyncratic, often reflecting the views of particular donors.[1] During the 1950s, the notions of systematizing student aid policies and working out ways to use scarce financial aid dollars to maximum advantage gained prominence. One impetus was the national recognition following the experience of the post–World War II GI Bill that broadening access to higher education was a more attractive and feasible goal for higher education than many observers had thought earlier. Another force for change was increasing competition for students among eastern colleges during the enrollment drought that followed after the Korean GI Bill in the mid-1950s. Colleges found themselves bidding against one another for students in ways that echo some recent developments, and they sought ways to bring some order to these competitive efforts and place some limits on them.

Out of these forces emerged in 1954 an entity called the College Scholarship Service (CSS), an offshoot of the College Entrance Examination Board, a long-standing cooperative effort of colleges and high schools to manage admissions policies. CSS was charged with developing a systematic methodology for determining objectively how much families in different financial circumstances could afford to pay for college. The analysis was to take into account family resources, including both income and assets, and family obligations, including number of children in the household, need to provide for retirement, and medical expenses. In effect, CSS was charged with designing a private taxation system that would determine how much of an additional dollar of family income could or should go toward college expenses and how much needed to come back to the family for living expenses. Although the formulas for determining these taxing rates have evolved over time, the system CSS evolved has in its essentials *Expected* remained in place, yielding a progressive tax on income and assets for *Family* college finance. *Contribution*

Accompanying these calculations of how much families could afford to pay for college was the development of a methodology for determining how the gap between college charges and family contributions should be met. CSS worked with colleges in developing an "aid-packaging" methodology built around the idea that students should be helped to meet their college financing needs with a combination of scholarship grants, educational loans, and work. The basic idea was that after being asked to shoulder a reasonable college workload and a tolerable burden of educational debt, the student's remaining need should be financed through grants. In the early years, the principal sources of these loan and grant funds were private, but an important feature of needs analysis and aid-packaging methodology was that it provided a handy framework within which state and federal grant, loan, and work programs could comfortably fit.

From the outset, a principal purpose of CSS's efforts was to encourage cooperation among higher education institutions in the determination of financial aid awards. CSS's principles urged that colleges should award aid only to students with demonstrated need and only to the extent of that need. Moreover, packaging approaches taken by schools should be consistent and equitable. As a means of both enforcing adherence to these principles and improving the accuracy of measurement of families' ability to pay, some schools joined together in "overlap groups," whose members systematically compared the financial aid files of student applicants whom they shared. The schools strove to reach agreement on their calculations of family ability to pay for these common applicants and thus presented a sort of united front to the families.

Underlying these prodigious efforts at calculation and coordination among the colleges was a rather powerful and attractive vision of the role of financial aid in U.S. higher education, a vision of such coherence and force that it might well be termed an "ideology." The vision suggested a way that the system of higher education, considered as a whole, could reconcile the claims of need and merit while achieving "equal educational opportunity" on a certain understanding of that notion. This vision presupposed that colleges and universities, with significant support from the government, would embrace a commitment to meet the full financial need of all their undergraduate students and to limit their financial aid to that purpose. They would simultaneously agree that admission of students would be without regard to ability to pay—admissions would be "need-blind." These commitments were to be honored in a higher education system marked by large differences in the prices, expenditures per student, and admissions selectivity of different schools, with the more selective schools being generally more expensive to attend and providing a more intensive education in terms of resources per student.

The governing idea was that with all schools agreeing on the same method for determining what families could pay and eliminating need as a factor in admissions decisions, price differences would be eliminated as a factor in the choice of college for all needy students. A family's choice among schools would be based purely on the educational and extracurricular merits of the various schools, judged by the family's lights. Schools at the same time would be exercising choice among students, through their policies of selective admission, only with regard to the student's qualities and not his or her ability to pay. Those students with the greatest "merit," as measured by high school achievements and test scores, would attend the "best," most selective schools, which provided the most educational resources. In this way, the claims of need were to be met by eliminating price as a factor in choice of school for needy students and the claims of merit were to be met by matching the most able and promising students with the best educational alternatives.

It is worth noting that this student-aid-driven vision of equity and merit was matched in public higher education by a parallel vision of education articulated in California's Master Plan. In this vision, the claims of need were to be met by keeping the price of public higher education in California low enough to be within reach of all. The colleges in the California system were to be sorted into three tiers, with differing levels of resource intensity and admissions selectivity. Students with the best high school credentials would be admitted to the prestigious University of California system; students with weaker academic qualifications would qualify for the State College (now State University) system, and the remainder of students would be eligible for the Community College system, which would provide both vocational postsecondary opportunities and preparation for transfer into the other tiers of the system after two years. Again here, need was to be addressed by keeping the price affordable for all, and merit was to be addressed by slotting students into different pieces of the system.

California's plan—stimulated by rapidly growing demand for higher education and premised on the burgeoning and seemingly boundless prosperity of that state—was imitated, often in less developed form, in a number of other states. The student-aid-inspired vision was driven mainly by private higher education and was never thought to be a realistic option without massive government support. For one thing, as we will discuss at length later, there are very large incentives for individual institutions to cheat on agreements to fund all the need of their applicants and that need alone. The truth is, most colleges and universities have never been financially able to fund the full need of their students. The schools that founded the College Scholarship Service were among the wealthiest in American higher education. The willingness of a larger community of institutions to embrace the principles of need-blind admission and full-need funding of aid was fueled in good part by the hope that governments would shoulder a substantial share of the burden of living up to those principles. A particularly handy by-product of the efforts of CSS was the ability to calculate "unmet need"— to see how many dollars it would take to fill the gap between what CSS determined that families could afford to pay and what the colleges and private philanthropy could make available.

And in fact, as we have noted, the needs analysis framework proved a very powerful instrument in building the case for public support of student aid. Many states adopted scholarship programs that keyed grant awards to levels of student need. As the federal government developed loan, grant, and work-study programs, they were all closely integrated with needs analysis principles. Thus the Pell grant system, introduced in 1972 as Basic Educational Opportunity Grants, incorporates its own need analysis formulas in determining both eligibility and award levels. Government-subsidized loans, work-study awards, and supplemental educational opportunity grants are all restricted to students with demonstrated need, and no student receiving such federal support may receive total support that exceeds his or her need level.

Indeed, in one of the ironies of the evolution of the student aid system, the federal government's increasing entanglement with private needs analysis systems has led it to assert increasing control over those systems, to the point where many significant elements of need analysis are now incorporated in federal law—a development that is not always for the best, given the powerful political forces that are brought to bear on definitions of ability to pay.

Student Aid in the System of Higher Education Finance

Although never coming close to full realization, the conception of a higher education system that meets the claims of need and merit through a combination of need-based student aid and selective college admission has had powerful effects in shaping both institutional and governmental policies toward higher education finance in the past four decades. The result has been a system of higher education unique in the world. It is a system characterized by an extraordinary degree of decentralization in governance and a remarkable variety in types of educational experiences offered. It is also characterized by very large differences across institutions in what higher education charges families and also, thanks to need-based student aid, by very large differences in what families at the same school pay for the same education.

Some sense of the scope and variety of the contemporary higher education scene can be obtained by reviewing some basic facts about enrollment and financing patterns.

In the fall of 1993, about 12.3 million individuals were enrolled as undergraduates in institutions of higher education in the United States (National Center for Education Statistics 1995a, tab. 172). Of that total, 7.2 million (58%) were full-time students and 5.1 million (42%) were part-time. The distribution across institutional types was as follows: there were 5.3 million undergraduates enrolled in public two-year colleges (43% of total undergraduate enrollment), 4.7 million enrolled in public four-year institutions (38%), and 2.3 million in private colleges and universities (19%).[2]

The distribution of full-time students across institutional categories was quite different. Only 1.9 million full-time undergraduates were enrolled at public two-year colleges (26% of total full-time undergraduate enrollment), with 3.5 million (49%) at public four-year schools and 1.8 million (25%) at private colleges and universities.

Financial aid figures importantly in the financing of college for many of these students, although its significance varies across sectors. Thus, for example, our analysis in Chapter 7 shows that in 1994, when the average sticker price for students at private research and doctorate-granting universities was about $15,000, the actual net amount paid by a typical student was only about $11,200. The difference for the average student was made up by about $600 in federal and state grants and over $3,000 in grants provided by the institution.[3]

These student aid subsidy dollars are spread unevenly among students. As we show in Chapter 3, low-income students at private institutions in 1993 received on average over $5,500 in grant aid, while upper income students received a nontrivial but still much smaller $1,500. At public institutions, student aid subsidies play a much smaller role. In 1994, tuition and fees at public research and doctorate-granting universities averaged almost $4,000. Of this total, a little over $600 was paid on average by state and federal grants, but public institutions contributed only $397 in institutional grants to the typical student, far less than the more than $3,000 provided by their private counterparts.

One reason for the difference between public and private higher education in the role of institutionally based student aid is that a great deal of the subsidy in public higher education is provided directly by state governments to the institutions. As reported in Chapter 7 (see Table 7.10), in 1994, 67% of revenues at public two-year colleges came from state and local appropriations, a figure that fell for public liberal arts colleges and public comprehensive universities (to around 57%) and bottomed out at 50% for public research and doctorate-granting universities (where 19% of revenues come from federal grants and contracts).[4] By contrast, net tuition revenue accounted for only 23% to 34% of all revenues at public colleges and universities. These basic numbers indicate that unlike the federal programs that target needy students, state and local appropriations have served primarily to keep tuition low for all students in public higher education. These appropriations remain the principal funding source.

The story is quite different in the private sector. Net tuition revenue comprises 55% of all revenues at private research and doctorate-granting universities, 76% of revenues at private liberal arts colleges, and 85% of revenues at private comprehensive universities. Even at the large private research universities (where federal grants and contracts account for 27% of revenues), tuition is by far the major revenue source in private higher education.

Federal involvement in student finance began to take something like its present shape in the 1960s and early 1970s. Aid in the form of grants and loans flows directly to students through the Pell and Stafford programs, while the so-called campus-based programs provide resources for colleges to distribute to needy students through grants, loans, and work. Following is a brief rundown on the major programs.[5]

Pell grants are awarded to needy undergraduate students who have not earned a bachelor's or professional degree. The maximum award for the 1995–96 academic year was $2,340; it will be $2,700 for 1997–98. The amount of the grant depends on the U.S. Department of Education's determination of an expected family contribution versus the cost of attendance at the school. Pell grant awards are either credited to school accounts or are paid directly to students.

Federal Stafford loans are the major form of self-help aid. Some are awarded directly by the government (for schools participating in the Direct Loan Program), and the rest are made through a bank or other lender backed by a federal guarantee. Some are subsidized and are awarded on the basis of need, and others are unsubsidized. Students may receive both subsidized and unsubsidized Stafford loans for the same enrollment period. Annual borrowing limits for dependent undergraduate students are $2,625 for first-year students, $3,500 for students in their second year, and $5,500 for students who have completed two years of study. Independent students (and dependent students who are unable to get a loan through the PLUS program, which provides federal loans to parents with good credit histories) can borrow considerably more, topping out at $10,500 a year for undergraduates who have completed two years of study. However, the total debt an undergraduate can have outstanding from all Stafford loans is $23,000 for a dependent student and $46,000 for an independent student. Interest on unsubsidized loans accumulates from the date of disbursal, although students have the option of deferring payment and capitalizing interest. The federal government pays the interest on subsidized loans while the individual is either an undergraduate or a graduate student and during a grace period after graduation. Among four repayment plans is an "income-contingent" payment option for Direct and Stafford loans, which keys the annual payment to the student's income.

Campus-based programs are administered directly by the financial aid offices at participating schools. There are three programs: the Federal Supplemental Educational Opportunity Grant (FSEOG) Program, which awards grants; the Federal Work-Study (FWS) Program, which offers jobs; and the Federal Perkins Loan Program, which offers loans. Eligibility in all three cases depends on financial need. FSEOG grants are aimed at students with exceptional financial need, and priority is given to students who also receive Pell grants. Maximum awards are $4,000 per year. FWS provides on- and off-campus jobs for undergraduate (and graduate) students, with salaries of at least the current federal minimum wage. Federal Perkins loans are low-interest loans (currently 5%) for students with exceptional financial need. Limits are $3,000 for each year of undergraduate study, up to a total of $15,000.

Chapter 3 (see Table 3.3) presents data on changes in funding for these programs over time. Briefly, in the 1994–95 academic year, $5.6 billion (in 1994 dollars) was spent on the Pell program, $24.3 billion on the federal Stafford loan program (guaranteed and direct loans), and $2.3 billion in the campus-based programs ($546 million in supplemental educational opportunity grants, $749 million in work-study, and $958 million in Perkins loans). It should be noted that the figures for the loan programs reflect the cost of outstanding loans and greatly overstate the amount of federal on-budget funds obligated for the loan program. In fiscal 1995, those amounts equaled $5.6 billion for guaranteed and direct loans (National Center for Education Statistics 1995a, tab. 353b).

Student aid is only one form in which governments help pay the costs of college. Federal research and development budgets support a large fraction of the costs of some universities, and state governments subsidize directly the public colleges and universities that they own and operate.

The most recent academic year for which we can pull together a complete picture of government contributions to higher education is 1992–93 (National Center for Education Statistics 1995a, tabs. 318–320). In that year, current-fund revenue for institutions of higher education totaled $170.9 billion. Of that total, state and local governments provided 27% of revenues ($45.7 billion), and the federal government provided only 12% ($21.0 billion).

When the federal contribution is limited to financial aid grants (as opposed to loans, research, and other support), the federal government share of current-fund revenue falls to only 2.8% (the value of Pell revenues in 1992–93 was $4.7 billion; National Center for Education Statistics 1995a, tab. 316).

Breaking the data down by sector, current-fund revenues at public colleges and universities equaled $108.2 billion, with Pell revenues accounting for $3.6 billion, or 3.4% of that total. At private colleges and universities, Pell revenues contributed a minuscule 1.7% ($1.0 billion) of $62.7 billion of current-fund revenue. To put these numbers in perspective, in 1992–93, the federal government spent $18.9 billion on its farm income stabilization program and $14.3 billion on elementary, secondary, and vocational education (U.S. Department of Commerce 1993, tab. 514.) The relatively limited role of federal dollars in the financing of higher education underscores the importance of thinking of higher education finance as a *national* and not only a *federal* problem and of attending to the behavior and interests of all the players—states and public and private institutions—when viewing the system and thinking about policy options.

Conclusion

The student aid system as it has evolved has had a considerable impact on the educational opportunities available to students and on the higher education attainment of Americans. Student aid, provided through both private and governmental sources, substantially reduces the net cost of higher education for many needy students—an effect suggested by the data reviewed here and covered in more detail in Chapter 3. Moreover, there is persuasive evidence that reducing the price lower-income students must pay significantly influences their decisions about attending college; indeed, it is clear that lower-income students are more sensitive to prices than other groups of students. It is also clear, as we report in Chapter 14, that the net effect of the system in both public and private higher education is to target more higher education subsidies on more highly qualified students—that is, the system does, in practice, "reward talent" as well as meet (some) need.

In retrospect, it is amazing that the system of needs analysis and need-based aid has been accepted as widely as it has. That American families, as belligerent as they are generally about paying taxes, would submit with relatively little complaint to the private taxation system of needs analysis is remarkable. Undoubtedly support for the system has been sustained by a widespread sense that this system has served goals of equal opportunity and of access to high-quality education.

These days, however, people's willingness to accept the vision of providing equal educational opportunity through need-based student aid has come increasingly into question at all levels. The president has recommended putting substantial federal resources—an annual amount greater than the cost of Pell—into tax credits and deductions for college tuition, a move that would lead the federal government abruptly away from its focus on need-based aid. Individual colleges and universities are increasingly vocal and unapologetic about awarding scholarships that fall out of the need-based system and also about tinkering with their need-based aid to get the most bang for the buck, rather than following impersonal rules. And state governments, increasingly unwilling or unable to finance the sort of ambitious vision embodied in California's Master Plan, are in many cases backing away from their commitment to low tuition without making the investments in their own need-based aid programs that could insulate needy students from the impact of higher tuition. Finally, families and students are increasingly dubious about the evenhandedness of the calculation of need-based aid, feeling that they should bargain with schools, that aid calculations may favor spendthrifts and tax cheats, and that the results of the system are ultimately arbitrary.

All these difficulties are exacerbated, if not caused, by the rapid changes in the strategic and financial environment facing American higher education. We turn to an examination of these changed circumstances in Chapter 2.

2

Changing the Rules

THE NEW STRATEGIC ROLE OF STUDENT AID

ABOUT A DECADE ago, the vice president for finance at a respected liberal arts college described over lunch an unfortunate but regrettably irremediable problem his institution had encountered. The school was, it seems, having trouble recruiting enough qualified students to fill its beds. The lowered enrollment led to excess capacity not just in the dorms but also in the dining halls and to some extent in the classrooms, as the load of students carried by a number of professors was smaller than it would have been with full enrollment. The result was a substantial revenue drain. The really unfortunate thing was that there were some good students out there eager to come to the school, but they couldn't afford to pay full tuition. They might have come with a reasonable tuition discount in the form of student aid, but the funds earmarked for student aid had been used up. With no money left for student aid, the institution was stuck.

Why not, his lunch partner inquired, increase the student aid budget to allow some of these would-be students to enroll at a discount? True, the school wouldn't get full payment for each enrollee, but since there was substantial excess capacity, adding these students would add little to costs, so whatever revenue was received would mostly be gravy.

Though intrigued by this argument, the financial VP quickly explained that the school just couldn't afford to spend any more on student aid. The student aid budget had been increasing faster than the rest of the college budget—by more than 10% per year—and the college had no choice but to set a firm ceiling to keep student aid costs from growing out of control. Now, in fact, that commitment to cost control was costing the college money—the additional students would have brought in additional net revenue. This was not something that the vice president, with his determined eye viewing the student aid office as a cost center, was prepared to see.

The simplest way to describe the change over the past decade in the way private colleges and universities approach student aid is to say that business officers, with few exceptions, don't think that way anymore. Rather than viewing student aid as a kind of charitable operation the college runs on the side, most private colleges and universities—and increasing numbers of public institutions—now regard student aid as a vital revenue management and enrollment management tool. Just as airlines have come to learn that a seat filled at a deep discount is a better deal than an empty seat, so colleges have come to see that a student with a big institutional grant still brings more net revenue than an empty seat in a classroom or an unoccupied bed in a dormitory.

The differences in how student aid is viewed that accompany this change in perspective go quite deep. It's useful to think in stylized terms of three "ideal types" of student aid operations. The first, which we might call the "need-blind, full-need" approach, is a fair description of reality at a handful of the best-endowed and most selective private colleges and universities in the nation. These are schools with long waiting lists of highly qualified full-pay customers. They could easily fill their freshman classes with little or no spending on student aid. For these schools, student aid is a real cost, reflecting a choice by the institution to give up revenue from full-pay students to change the profile of the freshman class, aiming perhaps at socioeconomic or racial diversity or honoring a more abstract principle of admitting students without ability to pay.[1] The very few institutions that are in this happy situation can afford to say and to mean that they admit students without regard to financial need and that they fund all such students to the extent of their need. The vision of the student aid system as guarantor of equal opportunity, described in Chapter 1, is alive and well at these schools, many of whom were indeed among the original architects of that vision.

A second ideal type of student aid operation, which might be called the "budget stretch" approach, would have fit a good number of private colleges and universities ten or fifteen years ago and more or less reflects the perspective of the vice president described at the start of this chapter. These institutions endorsed the same vision of student aid as the elite institutions with the "need-blind, full-need" approach but lacked the endowment resources and the affluent applicant pool to operate as the elite places did. These schools would budget what they felt they could for student aid and would stretch those student aid funds as best they could, trying to fill their freshman class with the best students they could, taking as little account as possible of ability to pay.

The third approach might be described as "strategic maximization." This outlook also fits schools that lack the resources of the most selective and best-endowed institutions. But now, instead of aiming to "stretch" a fixed student aid budget as far as possible, the school sets out deliberately to shape a financial aid strategy that maximally advances the combined (and conflicting) goals of admitting the best students and gaining as much revenue from them as possible.

In its full glory, strategic maximization can be a pretty ruthless business. If a student is willing to travel a long distance to be interviewed on campus, that can be a signal that the student is eager to attend, so it may be worth making a smaller financial aid offer to such a student while throwing more dollars at the young person who is more indifferent about attending one place or another. Students with an interest in a popular major may get smaller student aid offers than those interested in a more obscure and hence more underenrolled subject. And of course, students with higher SATs or a better jump shot, because they may attract applications from other full-pay students or may fill the stands at the stadium, are likely to get better aid offers than their less qualified colleagues.

Few schools have gone all the way down the road to this strategic maximization approach. But it is fair to say that the number of institutions following the "need-blind, full-need" strategy—always a small number—has shrunk in the past decade and that most institutions have moved their financial aid operations from the direction of the second category significantly toward the strategic maximization camp.

It is important to point out that this growing strategic emphasis did not come about because colleges have lost their moral compass or because college presidents have lost confidence in the professionalism of their financial aid offices. Rather, it is the *environment* of colleges and universities that has changed. Intense competition among colleges and universities for dollars and students has inevitably made student financial aid a strategic variable in maintaining institutions' financial health.

One source of intensified competition has been the demographic trend of the past two decades. Higher education has had to survive a reduction over the past twenty years of more than 20% in the number of people reaching age 18 every year, as the baby boomers moved through the college years and the baby bust succeeded them. This source of pressure is beginning gradually to attenuate as the children of the baby boom reach college age. However, the recovery from the trough is coming much more gradually than did the decline.[2]

Exacerbating the competitive pressures have been some broad financial trends over the past decade. As we show in detail in Part Two, both state and federal governments have supplied decreasing shares of higher education revenue over that period, and colleges and universities have made up the slack by increasing the share of revenues provided by parents and students in the form of tuition. At the same time, and partly as a reaction to higher tuition, colleges and universities have been under pressure from trustees and the general public to manage themselves more efficiently and to think more like businesses. Usually what the public and the trustees have in mind by this is more attention to cost-cutting, but higher education institutions have as well or instead drawn the lesson from the private sector that managing the customer base and squeezing as much revenue from customers as possible is also good business.

As colleges have come to appreciate better the strategic significance of financial aid, they have also changed the institutional structures through which aid is managed. When aid was seen as a charitable sideline, most institutions were content to leave the details to the professionals in the student aid office, with the main high-level concern being that of keeping the aid operation within budget. Student aid officers, who had collaborated on developing the elaborate needs analysis apparatus that governed the allocation of need-based student aid, formed strong professional and ethical bonds and developed both a rather inaccessible professional jargon and something of a tradition of holding their operation aloof from institutional goals.

These days, financial aid policy and practice at private and public institutions alike is frequently the province of high-level consultants and close presidential attention. Following on the heels of their colleagues in the admissions office, financial aid officers have come to find their duty hazardous, with a high level of accountability for results in terms of meeting institutional goals and limited patience for qualms based on professional ethics.

Strategic uses of student aid can take many forms, depending on an institution's goals and the tools available. These techniques will come in for detailed discussion in Parts Three and Four. At this point, we can simply note the key loci of decision in shaping financial aid strategies. The first broad choice is whether to confine aid offers to students with demonstrated financial need and, if so, to limit those offers to the extent of need. So-called no-need or merit aid involves awarding aid to students the school finds attractive, even if they have no need, or awarding aid in excess of their demonstrated need. But merit aid as such is only the tip of the iceberg, because colleges can and do vary the quality of the aid packages they offer to needy students according to how eager they are to attract the student. A typical student aid "package" offered to a student's family includes a financial aid grant, a loan, and a work-study job. It's not uncommon for two students with equivalent ability to pay enrolling at the same school to receive very different packages. One might have a $9,000 grant, a

$4,000 loan, and the expectation of earning $1,500 through work during the school year, while another might have a $14,500 grant with no loan or earnings expectation. The difference can be accounted for through the fact that the second student had a higher SAT score or some other attribute that the college found more attractive. Such "merit within need" is a major factor in student aid practices at a great many institutions that have no explicit merit or no-need aid.[3] Schools must also decide whether to take financial need into account in deciding which students to admit and whether to meet the full need of all the students they do admit. Variations and combinations of these strategies are almost endless and provide employment for a growing army of consultants. In Parts Three and Four, we will investigate their implications for the opportunities available to individual students and for the fairness and effectiveness of the higher education system. At this point, however, we should pause to note that although both public and private higher education are caught up in strategic thinking about student aid, they come at the problem in different ways owing to important differences in their institutional incentives.

Public and Private Higher Education:
Different Forces at Work

The key forces influencing public and private higher education in recent years are very different. The dominant force affecting public higher education has been the fiscal squeeze imposed by state governments. This fiscal squeeze predates the recession of the early 1990s and has persisted even through economic recovery. There is no reason to expect any abrupt reversal of this fiscal pressure on public universities. States have many high-priority needs, particularly in elementary and secondary education and in health care, and there is little reason to think that voters will reverse their antipathy to tax increases. The net effect of this financial squeeze has been a double whammy for needy students in many states: public tuitions have risen even as state-funded student aid has declined. Since federal funding for student aid has not expanded fast enough to make up this gap, access even to public higher education is becoming increasingly problematic for low-income students in many states. As we will discuss further in Part Two, these funding trends also affect choice within public higher education: in many states, it is the public community colleges that have held tuitions down, with the result that state colleges and public universities are increasingly out of reach for economically disadvantaged students.

Historically, in most states, individual public institutions have had rather little discretion over the tuition and fees they charge and have devoted few resources to institutionally based student aid. The financial aid operations in most state universities and colleges have thus been geared principally to doling out student aid funds earmarked by state and federal governments for that purpose. Interestingly, in that context, the main aim of the financial aid operation is to hand out as much money as possible—to adopt the most tolerant permissible measurement of need and to qualify students for as many grants as possible. This difference in perspective has in fact historically been a significant source of conflict between the student aid communities in public and private higher education. Private institutions, much of whose aid resources are internal, have had strong incentives to make calculations of need stringent, while public institutions have had the opposite incentive. This has begun to change, however, as higher tuitions in many states give some public institutions more discretionary funds that they can devote to aid. As this comes about, the same incentives to conserve aid resources and to use them strategically for enrollment and revenue management arise in the public sector as they have in the private. Supporting this trend has been an increasing push by public institutions to gain more control over their tuition and financial aid policies, as well as more ability to capture for their own purposes the revenues those policies generate. It is a key question, discussed in Part Four, whether this growing institutional discretion will be used to fund more need-based aid or whether the trend toward rapid growth in merit aid at public institutions will continue.

Private higher education has been subject to quite a different set of forces. The long period of demographic decline, coupled with the availability in many states of relatively low-priced public alternatives, has forced private colleges and universities to sell hard. Institutions have to spend money to preserve and enhance their image of quality but at the same time feel great pressure to make their product affordable to students who are interested in attending. Hence, the growing emphasis on strategic use of student aid: it provides a way of capturing the tuition revenue needed to preserve quality and its symbols while offering to as many students as possible a net price they find affordable. The operative idea here is *selective* price discounting, offering lower prices to families who are unwilling to pay more and especially to able students whose enrollment can enhance the reputation of the school.

As we shall see, this market situation poses a particularly vexing problem for the less affluent and less selective private institutions. In the United States a handful of highly selective, highly successful, and very rich private colleges and universities set a standard on class size, research reputation of faculty, course load, scientific facilities, and gymnasium equipment. Less affluent schools try to emulate the product of the leading institutions while lacking the endowment resources and deep applicant pools that the market leaders enjoy. These less affluent institutions find themselves judged not only on the basis of their ability to deploy these costly resources but also on their ability to recruit a student body with impressive qualifications. Needing to attract every dollar of revenue they can get and every high-quality student they can find, these institutions are under enormous pressure to use their financial aid resources effectively, through aggressive packaging policies and increasingly through explicit merit aid.

In this context, it is hard not to notice a touch of self-righteousness in the insistence of the most affluent and selective schools on the principles of need-blind admissions, full-need financing of admitted students, and no merit aid. In one sense, because the elite institutions use their large endowments to subsidize the education of all their students, they offer a substantial merit scholarship to every student they admit. Competing schools with fewer resources can with some justification claim that they are merely using their targeted merit scholarships to try to keep up. Moreover, even for very well endowed institutions, their ability to provide full funding for their needy students depends heavily on having a great many high-quality applicants who are willing and able to pay the sticker price. Put more bluntly, what differentiates schools that use merit aid or other strategically oriented aid strategies from those that don't is not mainly a difference in their moral fiber but in the number of top-quality full-pay students they are able to attract without such devices.

Conclusion

Intensifying competition for students, especially for affluent students with strong academic credentials, raises difficult policy questions for individual colleges and universities and for society. Individual institutions must weigh the potential advantages in prestige and student recruitment that may result from a successful merit scholarship program against the risks of getting caught up in a self-destructive zero-sum competition with other institutions for the same small set of students. Policy analysts must be concerned with the declining capacity of existing sources of need-based aid to provide the access to and choice in higher education that have been the cornerstones of national (both state and federal) higher education policy. They must also contemplate the implications of a growing commitment to non-need-based aid among institutions in both sectors, even as funding for need-based aid seems increasingly inadequate. We take up these problems in the remainder of this book.

Part Two

STUDENT AID AND EDUCATIONAL OPPORTUNITY: ARE WE KEEPING COLLEGE AFFORDABLE?

In our 1991 book (McPherson and Schapiro 1991b), we examined whether our nation's colleges and universities were affordable for Americans of all economic and social backgrounds and outlined policies aimed at the efficient allocation of government and private resources toward that aim. Here we review, update, and expand our earlier analysis. Of particular interest is how the combination of government funding and institutional financial and scholarship aid combine to explain observed trends in student access and choice.

We begin in Chapter 3 with an overview of changes over time in the finances of American colleges and universities, focusing on the role of governments, institutions, and families in meeting college costs. From the early 1960s until the early 1980s, the story was one of growing public commitments to the finance of higher education. From the mid-1980s on, one sees a reversal of this trend toward expanded government support of colleges. As the share of college costs financed by the federal government and even more by state governments has fallen, the share borne by families has inevitably increased.

Yet despite this apparent decline in affordability, the rates at which young people are enrolling in college have actually risen in recent years. We therefore turn in Chapter 4 to a consideration of the implications of these recent financing trends for the issue of access to college for people of all economic backgrounds. Our focus here is on the bearing of these recent trends in enrollment and pricing on our understanding of the impact of prices and student aid on the demand for college enrollment.

That enrollment rates have risen in the face of rising net prices for college suggests that college is, in some sense, remaining affordable. Yet it is important to consider not only whether but where students go to college, and we therefore proceed in Chapter 5 to examine evidence on the enrollment destinations of students from different income groups. Our findings here are not so reassuring, in that they indicate that students' choices about where to go to school seem to be increasingly constrained by finances.

Chapter 6 concludes with some speculations about the future and some observations about public policy.

3

Prices and Aid

THE GROWING BURDEN ON FAMILIES

TABLES 3.1 and 3.2 present a long-run view on college finance, containing data from selected years between 1939 and 1993. Table 3.1 shows how colleges' principal sources of revenue have changed over the past half century. For public institutions, state and local government spending has been the primary revenue source (accounting for more than half of revenues), with tuition providing a much smaller share (no more than a quarter of revenues). For private institutions, by contrast, tuition has by far been the principal source of revenue (accounting for between 43% and 57% of revenues).

This long view allows us to put recent changes in historical perspective. For public institutions, the contribution of state and local government spending has been declining for more than a decade, reaching its lowest postwar level (53%) in the most recent year for which we have data. While there has been a slight increase in the contribution of gifts and endowment earnings (from 3% to 6%), a much more important change has been the increased role of tuition (from 13% to 24%). Tuition at private institutions has also taken its largest role in forty years (going from 45% in 1955–56 to 54% in 1992–93) as the contribution of federal funding has declined to its lowest level since the late 1950s (falling from a peak of 30% in 1965–66 to 19% in 1992–93).

The pattern here is clear: tuition has been replacing government spending at both public and private institutions. Indeed, the pattern of revenue shares in the 1990s looks more like that of the late 1940s than that of any intervening decade.

Table 3.2 reports revenue shares for the major categories given in Table 3.1, averaged over public and private institutions, and also breaks down gross tuition by its sources, showing the share paid by families directly and the shares paid by various forms of student aid.

The most striking trend is the steady decline through 1980 in the overall share of tuition paid by families, the result of an increase in the enrollment share of public institutions, the growth of federal grants and contracts, and the rise in financial aid. However, the de-

TABLE 3.1
**Shares of Educational and General Revenue, Public and Private
Institutions, Selected Academic Years, 1939–1993 (%)**

| Academic Year | Gross Tuition | Government | | Gifts and Endowment Earnings | Other |
		Federal	State and Local		
Public Institutions					
1939–40	0.20	0.13	0.61	0.04	0.01
1949–50	0.25	0.13	0.56	0.03	0.03
1955–56	0.13	0.17	0.62	0.04	0.04
1959–60	0.13	0.21	0.59	0.04	0.03
1965–66	0.14	0.23	0.54	0.03	0.05
1969–70	0.15	0.19	0.57	0.03	0.05
1975–76	0.16	0.18	0.61	0.03	0.02
1979–80	0.15	0.16	0.62	0.04	0.03
1985–86	0.18	0.13	0.61	0.05	0.03
1989–90	0.20	0.13	0.58	0.05	0.04
1991–92	0.22	0.14	0.55	0.06	0.03
1992–93	0.24	0.14	0.53	0.06	0.04
Private Institutions					
1939–40	0.55	0.01	0.03	0.38	0.03
1949–50	0.57	0.12	0.04	0.23	0.05
1955–56	0.45	0.18	0.02	0.28	0.06
1959–60	0.43	0.25	0.02	0.25	0.05
1965–66	0.43	0.30	0.02	0.18	0.06
1969–70	0.44	0.26	0.03	0.19	0.08
1975–76	0.48	0.25	0.04	0.19	0.04
1979–80	0.47	0.25	0.04	0.19	0.05
1985–86	0.50	0.22	0.03	0.19	0.06
1989–90	0.51	0.21	0.04	0.18	0.06
1991–92	0.53	0.20	0.04	0.17	0.06
1992–93	0.54	0.19	0.04	0.17	0.06

Notes: 1992–93 data are preliminary. Figures in table do not include revenue from auxiliary enterprises or from sales and services. Government figures do not include student aid (which is included under gross tuition).

Sources: McPherson and Schapiro 1991b, p. 21; National Center for Education Statistics 1995a, tabs. 319, 320.

cline in the share of higher education revenues provided by families came to an abrupt halt in the 1980s, with the family share increasing by 8 percentage points in the 1979–80 to 1992–93 period (reaching the highest level, 22%, since 1959–60).

ABLE 3.2

hares of Higher Education Revenue, by Source, Selected Academic Years, 1939–1993 (%)

		Sources of Gross Tuition Revenue				Nontuition Revenue		
cademic Year	Gross Tuition	Families	Institutions	Federal Government	State Government	Federal Grants	State and Local Grants	Gifts and Endowment Earnings
⟩39–40	0.37	0.35	0.02	0.00	0.00	0.07	0.33	0.21
⟩49–50	0.40	0.37	0.03	0.00	0.00	0.12	0.32	0.12
⟩59–60	0.26	0.22	0.03	0.00	0.01	0.23	0.34	0.13
⟩65–66	0.26	0.21	0.04	0.00	0.01	0.26	0.33	0.09
⟩69–70	0.25	0.20	0.04	0.00	0.01	0.22	0.38	0.08
⟩75–76	0.26	0.16	0.04	0.04	0.02	0.20	0.43	0.08
⟩79–80	0.26	0.14	0.04	0.06	0.02	0.19	0.43	0.09
⟩85–86	0.29	0.17	0.05	0.05	0.02	0.16	0.41	0.10
⟩89–90	0.31	0.19	0.05	0.05	0.02	0.16	0.37	0.10
⟩91–92	0.34	0.22	0.05	0.05	0.02	0.16	0.35	0.10
⟩92–93	0.35	0.22	0.06	0.05	0.02	0.16	0.33	0.10

Notes: 1992–93 data are preliminary. Both veterans' educational benefits and Social Security benefits paid to ialified college students are excluded from federal tuition payments.
Sources: McPherson and Schapiro 1991b, p. 23; National Center for Education Statistics 1995a, tab. 318; College ⟩ard 1995, tab. 1.

Table 3.2 also underscores that it is the states rather than the federal government whose role is changing most dramatically. As late as 1979–80, state governments contributed 45% of all of higher education revenues, almost all of it through direct support of state-run institutions. By 1992–93, that share had fallen to 35% and has almost certainly fallen further since. The share of higher education revenues supplied by federal student aid has remained roughly constant since the mid-1970s, but the share provided by federal research support has declined substantially (from 26% to 16%) from its high in the mid-1960s. Since research support is concentrated in a fairly small number of institutions, this decline is of major importance for that subgroup.

We turn now to a detailed look at changes in the sources of financial aid. Table 3.3 shows the overall magnitudes of federal and other forms of student aid, expressed in constant 1994 dollars, for selected years since 1963. With respect to how federal funding has developed, the period from 1963 to the present can be usefully divided into four subperiods. Before 1975, a fairly modest total of "generally available" aid was divided between guaranteed loans and the so-called campus-based programs, which provide funds for institutions to use for student aid in the form of grants, loans, and work.[1] From 1975 to 1980, generally available aid grew rapidly (doubling in real dollars between 1975–76 and 1980–81), with substantial expenditures on the newly

TABLE 3.3
Aid Awarded to Students, by Source, Selected Academic Years, 1963–1995 (millions of 1994 dollars)

	1963–64	1970–71	1975–76	1980–81	1985–86	1990–91	1992–93	1993–94	1994–95
Federal programs									
Generally available aid									
Pell grants	0	0	2,505	4,088	4,866	5,436	6,427	5,731	5,570
Supplemental educational opportunity grants	0	499	538	630	559	501	576	572	546
State student incentive grants	0	0	53	124	103	65	74	73	72
Work-study	0	849	789	1,131	895	806	812	782	749
Perkins loans	547	898	1,231	1,188	959	964	928	932	958
Guaranteed and direct loans	0	3,791	3,389	10,623	12,056	14,034	15,523	21,480	24,325
Subtotal	547	6,038	8,505	17,784	19,439	21,806	24,340	29,571	32,221

Specially directed aid								
Social Security	0	1,864	2,924	3,225	0	0	0	0
								0
Veterans	322	4,187	11,182	2,936	1,178	752	1,079	1,209	1,390
Military	201	241	259	344	467	408	409	411	415
Other grants	42	59	169	209	92	130	169	170	184
Other loans	0	157	120	106	508	382	428	462	400
Subtotal	565	6,508	14,654	6,820	2,245	1,672	2,085	2,252	2,388
Total federal aid	1,112	12,546	23,159	24,604	21,684	23,479	26,425	31,823	34,610
State grant programs	269	882	1,311	1,372	1,788	2,059	2,212	2,408	2,628
Institutional and other grants	1,297	3,125	3,126	2,782	4,040	6,379	7,788	8,349	8,929
Total federal, state, and institutional aid	2,678	16,553	27,596	28,758	27,512	31,917	36,425	42,580	46,167

Note: 1993–94 and 1994–95 data are preliminary.
Sources: McPherson and Schapiro 1991b, p. 26; College Board 1995, tabs. 2, B.

introduced Pell program, the means-tested grant program put in place under the Nixon administration in 1974. From 1980 to 1992, both the Pell program and guaranteed loans increased at a slower rate (with around a 50% real increase in each). Since that time, growth in guaranteed and direct loans has been enormous (a 57% real increase between 1992–93 and 1994–95), but expenditures on the Pell program have fallen by 13% in real dollars. Thus even though federal aid in 1994–95 totaled $34.6 billion, up from $23.5 billion in 1990–91 (in 1994 dollars), virtually all of the increase was in the form of loans rather than grants.

The real value of state grants has followed a positive trend throughout the entire period, but the absolute increase has been dwarfed by the growth in institutional grants. The real value of institutional grants has more than tripled over the past fifteen years, going from $2.8 billion in 1980–81 (in 1994 dollars) to $8.9 billion in 1994–95.

These aggregate aid numbers provide only limited insight into how student aid has helped particular groups of students meet the costs of college. One useful bit of insight into this question is provided by Table 3.4, which examines changes over time in the targeting of the federal Pell program.

Whereas in the early years of the program, most grant recipients were traditional-aged college students supported by their parents (in 1973–74, only 13% of Pell recipients were independent students), by 1985–86 the majority of recipients were independent students. That percentage has been fairly stable at around the 60% level during the 1990s.

Equally striking changes have occurred in the distribution of Pell funds between the nonprofit and proprietary sectors. From 1973–74 to 1987–88, there was a remarkable increase (from 7% to 27%) in the share of Pell funds going to students attending proprietary vocational and technical institutions, most of which offer nondegree programs of less than two years.[2] Since that time, however, a tightening of federal aid guidelines has lowered that share all the way to 15%, the lowest level since the early 1980s. Although fully comparable data are not available for federal loans, it is clear that there has been a similar reversal of the trend toward an increasing share of loans going toward proprietary institutions. This is a quite striking turnabout in a situation that had garnered enormous attention in public discussions of higher education finance in the early 1990s.

Tables 3.1 through 3.4 provide an overall picture of changes over time in the financing of American higher education. What is missing is an analysis of the different prices charged to students from differ-

TABLE 3.4

Distribution of Pell Grant Funds to Independent Students and Proprietary Schools, Selected Academic Years, 1973–1994 (%)

Academic Year	Recipients Who Are Independent Students	Revenue to Students at Proprietary Institutions
1973–74	13.3	7.0
1975–76	29.8	9.0
1977–78	38.5	8.9
1979–80	33.8	10.5
1981–82	41.9	13.5
1983–84	47.5	18.8
1985–86	50.4	22.2
1987–88	57.5	26.6
1989–90	59.0	23.1
1991–92	61.5	20.7
1992–93	62.1	18.5
1993–94	59.2	15.3

Note: 1993–94 data are preliminary.

Sources: McPherson and Schapiro 1991b, p. 28; College Board 1995, tabs. 5, 7.

ent income backgrounds, along with the federal, state, and institutional aid available to them.

Fortunately, National Postsecondary Student Aid Surveys covering the 1986–87 and 1992–93 academic years provide detailed student-level data on higher education financing. Figures 3.1, 3.2, and 3.3 present a graphical representation of data contained in Table 3.5. Figure 3.1 shows the distribution of gross tuition costs (in 1992–93 dollars) for full-time, dependent students attending private nonprofit colleges and universities during each of the survey years. Students are divided into low-, middle-, and high-income groups based on the following income breakdowns:

Income Group	1986–87	1992–93
Low	< $23,500	< $30,000
Middle	$23,500–$54,900	$30,000–$70,000
High	> $54,900	> $70,000

These income brackets are equivalent in 1992–93 dollars, reflecting the 27.6% increase in prices between the academic years being compared.

TABLE 3.5
Financing of Undergraduate Tuitions, 1986–87 and 1992–93
(in 1992–93 dollars)

Family Income Category		Net Tuition	Federal Grants	Federal Loan Subsidies	State Grants	Institutional Grants	Gross Tuition
Private Nonprofit Institutions							
Low	1986–87	1,372	1,585	958	1,354	1,780	7,049
	1992–93	3,619	1,628	1,141	982	2,942	10,312
Middle	1986–87	4,048	355	840	582	1,754	7,579
	1992–93	7,704	184	750	328	2,919	11,886
High	1986–87	7,390	117	317	92	719	8,635
	1992–93	11,622	23	304	55	1,388	13,391
Public Institutions							
Low	1986–87	−439	980	370	355	168	1,434
	1992–93	360	1,051	489	352	267	2,520
Middle	1986–87	1,030	97	278	102	154	1,661
	1992–93	2,113	84	220	85	263	2,765
High	1986–87	1,721	37	73	18	83	1,932
	1992–93	3,112	11	84	38	193	3,437
Private For-Profit Institutions (Proprietary Schools)							
Low	1986–87	1,124	1,546	1,233	266	70	4,238
	1992–93	4,155	1,254	1,102	122	69	6,702
Middle	1986–87	3,281	180	1,245	207	105	5,018
	1992–93	5,842	94	784	69	110	6,898
High	1986–87	4,630	33	349	27	62	5,102
	1992–93	6,852	7	188	0	25	7,071

Note: Numbers are averages for all full-time, dependent students attending a particular institutional type.

Source: Calculated using data from National Postsecondary Student Aid Surveys databases.

There was a considerable real increase in gross tuition charges (sticker prices) for students from all income backgrounds, with the largest absolute increase for high-income students. However, increases in the net tuition price actually paid by students were somewhat smaller than increases in sticker prices at private institutions: $4,232 versus $4,756 for high-income students, $3,656 versus $4,307 for middle-income students, and $2,247 versus $3,263 for low-income students.

Federal grants remained approximately constant in real value for low-income students attending private institutions, which, in light of the considerable real increase in gross tuition, means that the percentage of tuition covered by federal financial aid for low-income stu-

Figure 3.1 Financing of Undergraduate Tuition at Private Nonprofit Institutions, 1986–87 and 1992–93.

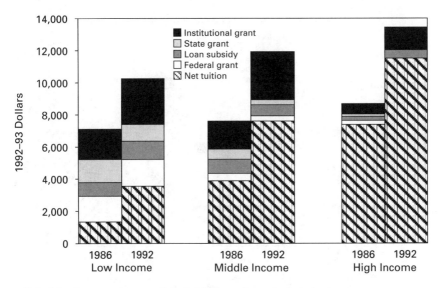

Note: Numbers are averages for all full-time, dependent students.
Source: National Postsecondary Student Aid Surveys.

dents has decreased considerably over time, from 22% in 1986–87 to only 16% in 1992–93. The real value of federal grants for more affluent students fell over the period, although federal grants account for a very small percentage of gross tuition for these students.

The subsidy value of federal loans (computed at 50% of the total loan amount; see McPherson and Schapiro 1991b) changed little over time, implying once again that federal financial aid accounts for a declining share of gross tuition. Not only do state grants contribute a decreasing share of gross tuition, but they have also declined significantly, especially for low-income students (for whom the real value of state grants fell by $372). Institutional grants, by contrast, have increased rapidly for students from all income groups, particularly for low- and middle-income students (with real increases of around $1,165, compared to an increase of $669 for high-income students). The percentage contribution of institutional grants to gross tuition has increased for students from all income groups—from 25% to 29% for low-income students, from 23% to 25% for middle-income students, and from 8% to 10% for high-income students.

Figure 3.2 provides analogous information for students attending public colleges and universities. As for private institutions, sticker

Figure 3.2 Financing of Undergraduate Tuition at Public Institutions, 1986–87 and 1992–93.

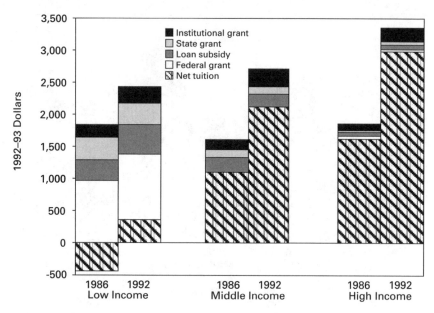

Note: Numbers are averages for all full-time, dependent students.
Source: National Postsecondary Student Aid Surveys.

prices increased in real terms for all groups. Again, increases in the net tuition price actually paid by students were somewhat smaller than increases in sticker prices for each income group: $1,391 versus $1,505 for high-income students, $1,083 versus $1,104 for middle-income students, and $799 versus $1,086 for low-income students. Note that for the average low-income student attending a public institution, the contribution of federal, state, and institutional aid exceeded the gross tuition price in 1986–87, implying a negative net tuition payment. This reflects the difference between gross tuition and gross total costs of attendance, the latter including room, board, and other charges. Thus the excess of financial aid over gross tuition is applied against other costs of attendance.

Federal grants for low-income students attending public colleges and universities increased slightly in real terms, but not enough to maintain the percentage contribution of these grants to gross tuition—the percentage of tuition covered by federal financial aid for low-income students decreased from 68% in 1986–87 to 42% in 1992–93. The subsidy value of federal loans, while increasing for low-

income students by $119 in real dollars, also failed to grow enough to
maintain its share of gross tuition (which fell from 26% to 19%). The
contribution of state grants also declined. Institutional grants, by contrast, increased for students from all income groups, although the percentage contribution of institutional grants to gross tuition is relatively small in public higher education (the largest contribution is for
low-income students, where it has been holding steady at around
11%).

Finally, Figure 3.3 presents information for students attending private for-profit (proprietary) schools. Again, sticker prices increased in
real terms for all groups, although in this case increases in the net
tuition price actually paid by students were larger than increases in
sticker prices for each income group: $2,222 versus $1,969 for high-
income students, $2,561 versus $1,880 for middle-income students,
and $3,031 versus $2,464 for low-income students. This reflects the
decline in the real value of financial aid from all sources, most notably
the fall in the real value of federal grants for low-income students and
the real decline in the subsidy value of federal loans for more affluent
students. Whereas the sum of federal grants and loans in 1986–87
accounted for 66%, 28%, and 7% of gross tuition for, respectively,
low-, middle-, and high-income students attending proprietary schools,
those contributions fell to 35%, 13%, and 3% in 1992–93.

The NPSAS data unfortunately take us only through 1992–93.
There is evidence of further important change in student financing
patterns since then, apparently largely the result of changes in the
federal student aid programs introduced in the 1992 reauthorization
of the Higher Education Act.

The most striking such change is the spectacular run-up in federal
loan volume since 1992–93. As we noted in Table 3.3, federal lending
has grown in real dollars by almost $9 billion in the two years be-
tween 1992–93 and 1994–95. Probably the most important explanation for this growth is a set of changes in needs analysis methodology
introduced in the 1992 reauthorization. Students receive interest subsidies on their loans only to the extent that they can be shown to have
financial need. Congress, which some years ago decided to write the
needs analysis rules itself rather than leaving them to student aid
experts, made those rules significantly more lenient for middle- and
upper-middle-income students in the 1992 legislation. Most strikingly,
a family's home equity was no longer counted as an asset. These
changes imply that many families at public institutions who would
not have qualified as needy under the old rules can now get subsidized loans. Other factors contributing to the loan run-up probably
include the rising costs at public institutions, which also qualify more

Figure 3.3 Financing of Undergraduate Tuition at Private For-Profit Institutions, 1986–87 and 1992–93.

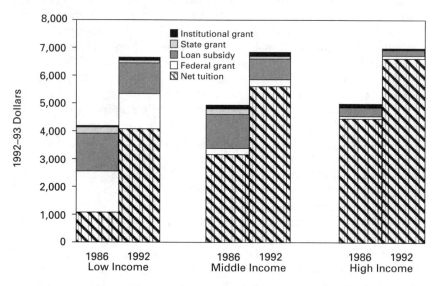

Note: Numbers are averages for all full-time, dependent students.
Source: National Postsecondary Student Aid Surveys.

students for loans, and the introduction of federal direct loans, which have simplified the process of obtaining a loan considerably.

This recent pattern of declining real funding for federal grants, coupled with rapid expansion in subsidized loans, seems not to reflect a deliberate policy shift but rather the working out of budgetary pressures. Since grant funds are a form of discretionary spending, their real decline reflects the impact of the general squeeze on the federal budget. Guaranteed loans, by contrast, are an entitlement and so are not affected in the same way in the short run by budget battles.

But intended or not, this shift has significant implications for the targeting of federal aid subsidies. Since Pell grant funds are very effectively targeted on low-income students, as the NPSAS data show, while federal loan subsidies are distributed much more broadly to middle-income as well as lower-income students, the shift of funding toward loans clearly moves support away from low-income students and toward the middle class.

4

Access

STUDENT RESPONSE TO HIGHER PRICES—
AND HIGHER RETURNS

OUR REVIEW OF pricing and aid makes clear that recent years have seen a substantial run-up in the costs to students of attending college, even after allowing for the effects of financial aid. These cost increases are widespread across types of institutions and family income levels of students. It is natural to expect that these substantial increases in college costs should produce a decline in rates of college attendance, yet, as we will show in a moment, enrollment rates of high school graduates are actually at an all-time high. The question before us is whether and how we can reconcile these trends with the econometric evidence that higher prices or lower aid levels tend to discourage college attendance.

First let's look at the facts. Table 4.1 traces changes over time in college enrollment rates for high school graduates from different races. Data are available for white students from 1960 but for blacks and Hispanics only from 1976. Due to the high variability reflecting small sample sizes for blacks and Hispanics, three-year moving averages are also calculated for those groups.

Beginning with whites, there was little trend between 1960 and 1980, with enrollment rates hovering at around the 50% level.[1] After that time, however, enrollment rates climbed to the 60% level in the late 1980s, continuing to rise to around 64% in the past few years. The moving average for blacks was around 45% in the late 1970s, fell to around 40% during the first half of the 1980s, and then regained that loss before ending the period with enrollment rates around the 50% level. Rates for Hispanics were generally slightly below 50% from 1977 to 1984 and fell during the mid-1980s before averaging around 55% over the subsequent period.

Thus enrollment rates for all three racial groups have risen in the 1990s. Enrollment rates are near record levels for all three racial groups, with a notable gain beginning around 1988 and continuing to the present. Yet we should also note that the gap between the enrollment rate of whites and those of blacks and Hispanics is larger now

TABLE 4.1
College Enrollment Rates of High School Graduates (%)

Year	Whites	Blacks	Three-Year Average	Hispanics	Three-Year Average
1960	45.8	—	—	—	—
1961	49.5	—	—	—	—
1962	50.6	—	—	—	—
1963	45.6	—	—	—	—
1964	49.2	—	—	—	—
1965	51.7	—	—	—	—
1966	51.7	—	—	—	—
1967	53.0	—	—	—	—
1968	56.6	—	—	—	—
1969	55.2	—	—	—	—
1970	52.0	—	—	—	—
1971	54.0	—	—	—	—
1972	49.4	—	—	—	—
1973	48.1	—	—	—	—
1974	47.1	—	—	—	—
1975	51.2	—	—	—	—
1976	48.9	41.9	—	52.6	—
1977	50.7	49.6	45.7	51.3	48.9
1978	50.1	45.7	46.9	42.9	46.3
1979	49.6	45.4	44.3	44.8	46.8
1980	49.9	41.8	43.4	52.7	49.9
1981	54.6	42.9	40.4	52.1	49.3
1982	52.0	36.5	39.3	43.1	49.8
1983	55.0	38.5	38.4	54.3	47.3
1984	57.9	40.2	40.3	44.3	49.9
1985	59.4	42.3	39.7	51.1	46.6
1986	56.0	36.5	43.6	44.4	43.0
1987	56.6	51.9	44.5	33.5	45.0
1988	60.7	45.0	49.9	57.0	48.6
1989	60.4	52.8	48.0	55.4	53.2
1990	61.5	46.3	48.2	47.3	53.3
1991	64.6	45.6	46.6	57.1	53.1
1992	63.4	47.9	49.7	54.8	58.1
1993	62.8	55.6	51.5	62.5	55.4
1994	63.6	50.9	—	48.9	—

Note: Enrollment rates reflect enrollment in college as of October of each year for individuals aged 16 to 24 who graduated from high school (including GED recipients) during the preceding twelve months.

Source: Based on data in National Center for Education Statistics 1995a, tab. 177.

than it was in the late 1970s. At that time, white enrollment rates were about 5 percentage points higher than those for blacks and about 3 percentage points higher than those for Hispanics. In the 1980s that gap widened, and in the early 1990s it was around 12 percentage points for blacks and 7 or so for Hispanics.

Which factors have contributed to the observed trends? Have changes in tuition and financial aid had an impact? Have government policies played a positive role?

The question of how pricing and aid influence student enrollment decisions has received much attention from economists and policy analysts over the past decade. One school of thought, led by Lee Hansen (1983), has focused on the difficulty of discerning much impact of changes over time in prices and in federal student aid policy on national enrollment trends. Certainly the coincidence of higher prices and higher enrollment rates in recent years that we have just noted could be used to buttress these arguments. Another school of thought has focused on econometric studies, relying mostly on cross-section data, that show significant negative effects of price on enrollment and significant positive effects of aid on enrollment.

Our own work (McPherson, Schapiro, and Winston 1993, ch. 8; McPherson and Schapiro 1991a; McPherson and Schapiro 1991b, ch. 3) presented new empirical results in an attempt to reconcile differences in the literature. We presented a properly controlled econometric analysis of time-series data that showed significant effects of aid on enrollment for students from lower-income families (defined as income below $20,000 in 1990 dollars).

This finding is very important: it provides an economic foundation for the considerable investments in financial aid made by federal and state governments as well as by institutions. Specifically, our results indicate that increases in net cost over time lead to decreases in enrollment rates for lower-income students. The magnitude of the coefficient on net cost implies that for lower-income students, a $150 net cost increase, expressed in 1993–94 dollars, results in a 1.6% decline in enrollment for that income group. A consensus in the econometric literature is that a $150 increase in net cost reduces enrollment rates by 1.8%. Our result is thus broadly consistent with typical cross-sectional findings and thus helps ease the worry that the historical evidence of the time-series studies is at odds with the best econometric work.

Though our findings corroborate the presence of a significant price or aid effect for low-income students, we found no evidence that increases in net cost inhibited enrollment for more affluent students. Thus policies that call for cross-subsidization of students—richer students paying a substantial share of educational and general costs with these revenues supporting discounts for lower-income students— makes sense from the viewpoint of economic efficiency.

A recent study by Tom Kane (1995) supports our findings. Kane examined the effect of public college tuition on college entry, with the bulk of the evidence pointing to large enrollment impacts, especially for low-income students and for those attending two-year colleges. Specifically, states with high public tuitions have lower college entry rates, the gap in enrollment between high- and low-income youth is wider in high-tuition states, and within-state tuition hikes lead to lower enrollment rates and wider gaps between high- and low-income youth.

Is it possible, then, to reconcile these econometric results with the recent growth of enrollment rates in the face of rising net costs? We think so, for several reasons.

First, of course, prices are not by any means the sole determinant of enrollment rates. There is strong evidence that the economic returns to investments in college have grown substantially in recent years, and this is an obvious explanation for the growth in college attendance. According to U.S. Bureau of the Census (1994) data, a worker with a bachelor's degree earned 1.54 times as much in 1975 as a worker with a high school diploma; in 1992, that ratio had risen to 1.74. Unfortunately, this growing labor market advantage for the college-educated came about mostly because of declines in the real incomes of recent high school graduates rather than because of large real gains for college attendees (see Katz and Murphy 1992). As Kane (1995) argues, this change in returns can go a long way toward explaining the increase in enrollment rates.

Moreover, the increase in enrollment rates has not been uniform across income groups. Kane (1995) notes that the gap in enrollment rates between students from the lowest-income quartile and those from the other three quartiles grew by 12 percentage points between 1980 and 1993 (p. 6). We noted earlier that the gap between the enrollment rate of whites and those of blacks and Hispanics have likewise grown over that period, a fact that is consistent with the lower average socioeconomic status of blacks and Hispanics. These results support the evidence in our econometric work that price sensitivity to enrollment is concentrated among low-income students, with little or no price response observed among higher-income students.

We can make this point more explicit by looking back at Table 3.5 and Figure 3.2. If we concentrate on public higher education, the sector that dominates the total enrollment numbers, it appears that net tuition increases of $1,100 to $1,400 for middle- and upper-income students have not been enough to deter enrollment in the face of high economic returns to college. Economists have long criticized the large subsidies to middle- and upper-income families implicit in the states' tendency to subsidize college attendance through low public tuition. This evidence is consistent with the judgment that at the margin, shifting some of the financing burden from state governments to middle- and upper-income families does not discourage enrollment.

However, the growing gap between enrollment rates for lower- and higher-income students suggests that increases in the net cost for low-income students do discourage college attendance. Kane's (1995) evidence that the gap between low-income and high-income enrollment rates by state is positively related to rates of growth in public tuition strongly suggests that the increases in net cost for low-income students shown in Table 3.5 are having an impact on their access.

These facts make the trend of the past few years to reduce real funding of Pell grants and increase funding for loans all the more unsettling. As we noted earlier, expanded loan funds since 1992–93 have probably gone largely to middle- and upper-middle-income students at public colleges and universities. While they no doubt welcome such support, there is little evidence that it is essential to enabling them to attend college. Yet federal grant dollars are very effectively targeted on low-income students, and there is evidence that changes in support for low-income students do influence their college-going. So the recent redistribution of federal dollars appears to be going the wrong way from the standpoint of both social equity and efficiency in promoting college enrollment.

One final point is worth noting. For-profit colleges have endured the largest impact on net prices for low-income students, as their tuitions have gone up and both grant and loan support have declined. It seems very likely that this dramatic change in their financial situation has had an important effect on both attendance levels and the financial well-being of many of these establishments. Unfortunately, we have no reliable database to draw on to study the fate of this intriguing sector.

5

Choice

HOW ABILITY TO PAY AFFECTS COLLEGE OPTIONS

WHEN WE CONSIDER the topic of educational opportunity, we take into account both the issue of the accessibility of higher education to lower-income students and the overall distribution of students across institutional types. Despite the concerns we have noted about the impact on access of the recent rise in college costs for low-income students, the high overall rates of college attendance in recent years point to considerable success in making *some* form of postsecondary education financially accessible to a very wide range of Americans. Although continuation of recent trends could easily threaten the nation's achievements in providing "access" to college, it is important to stress the considerable success of the U.S. system in making it possible for so many Americans to continue their education beyond high school.

Yet the existing financing system may be much less successful in providing a *suitable* postsecondary experience for many disadvantaged students. The range of alternatives available to students appears to be quite sharply constrained by their income under existing arrangements. In most states, community colleges are the cheapest and most accessible alternative for low-income students, a fact that is reflected in their disproportionate representation in these institutions. Although the issue of "choice" is often expressed in terms of public versus private alternatives, opportunity to attend a flagship public university or indeed any four-year public institution is importantly constrained by income in many states.

It is interesting to note that much of the popular discussion regarding where students go involves middle-income students, not lower-income students. It is often suspected that students from middle-income backgrounds have been most affected by the considerable real increases in tuition at private colleges and universities. Students from lower-income backgrounds qualify for need-based financial aid, lessening the chance that these students experience an affordability problem. Students from upper-income backgrounds receive a different but analogous form of financial aid—parental contributions that do not require major proportions of available annual incomes. But, the story goes, when tuitions rise faster than other economic indicators, students from middle-income backgrounds are forced to switch to less costly educational alternatives.[1]

Here we examine changes over time in the higher education destination for students of different economic backgrounds. This allows us not only to consider the "middle-income melt" topic but also to examine the broader question of who goes where and how that compares with decades past.

Our analysis relies on data from an annual survey of first-time, full-time college freshmen, the American Freshman Survey. These data are self-reported by students, thereby undoubtedly introducing measurement error. Nevertheless, we use these data for two reasons. First, they are the only consistently reported annual data on the college choices of students from different income backgrounds. Second, there is no reason to expect the biases in student reporting of income to vary systematically over time. So even though the data may be inaccurate in a particular year, their variation over time should be fairly reliable. Therefore, though we discuss the distribution of students by income at a given time, we focus more on changes over time in that distribution.

Our first step is to disaggregate income distribution data into reasonable groupings that can be traced over time. The most recent available survey data are from the fall of 1994, during which time students were asked to report parents' income for 1993. We have created six basic income brackets from those data (lower, lower-middle, middle, upper-middle, upper, and richest) and computed their constant-dollar equivalents in a previous survey year, 1980. The 1994 income bands almost perfectly approximate constant-dollar equivalents for those used in 1980.[2] The income groupings from the questionnaires are as follows:[3]

Income Group	1980	1994
Lower	< $10,000	< $20,000
Lower-middle	$10,000–$15,000	$20,000–$30,000
Middle	$15,000–$30,000	$30,000–$60,000
Upper-middle	$30,000–$50,000	$60,000–$100,000
Upper	$50,000–$100,000	$100,000–$200,000
Richest	> $100,000	> $200,000

Table 5.1 presents data on the distribution of students from different income backgrounds across institutional types.[4] The institutional types are private universities, private four-year colleges, private two-year colleges, public universities, public four-year colleges, and public

TABLE 5.1
Freshman Enrollment, by Income Background, across Institution Types (%)

Institution Type	Income Background						
	Lower	Lower Middle	Middle	Upper Middle	Upper	Richest	All Grou
1994							
Private university	2.6	3.3	3.9	6.6	13.2	22.4	5.7
Four-year	12.8	15.3	16.6	18.4	22.2	27.3	17.1
Two-year	3.1	2.9	2.5	2.2	2.8	3.8	2.7
All private	18.5	21.5	23.0	27.2	38.2	53.5	25.5
Public university	10.9	14.5	18.1	24.9	27.8	24.6	19.1
Four-year	23.2	24.6	25.2	25.9	20.1	13.3	24.1
Two-year	47.3	39.4	33.7	22.1	13.9	8.6	31.3
All public	81.4	78.5	77.0	72.9	61.8	46.5	74.5
Total	100.0	100.0	100.0	100.0	100.0	100.0	100.0
1980							
Private university	2.2	2.9	3.9	6.8	12.8	19.8	5.2
Four-year	13.4	15.1	15.8	17.7	25.2	31.7	16.8
Two-year	5.6	5.1	3.7	3.3	2.6	2.5	4.0
All private	21.2	23.1	23.4	27.8	40.6	54.0	26.0
Public university	10.1	13.2	17.4	24.6	26.6	19.6	18.1
Four-year	22.8	21.3	20.4	20.1	15.6	11.9	20.2
Two-year	45.9	42.4	38.9	27.6	17.3	14.5	35.8
All public	78.8	76.9	76.7	72.3	59.5	46.0	74.1
Total	100.0	100.0	100.0	100.0	100.0	100.0	100.0

Source: Calculated from results from the American Freshman Survey.

two-year colleges. Figures for all private institutions and all public institutions are also provided.

In 1994, some 25.5% of students attended private institutions. That figure represents a very small drop from 26.0% in 1980. Thus our data do not indicate a significant long-term downward trend in the percentage of full-time students attending private colleges and universities. With total first-time, full-time freshman enrollment in 1994 of around 1.5 million, a decline of ½ percentage point between 1980 and 1994 represents only about 7,500 fewer freshmen enrolled in private institutions relative to what would have occurred had the private share remained at the 1980 level.[5] Looking within the private sector, the share of all students attending private universities has held rather steady over time, starting at 5.2% and ending in 1994 at 5.7%. The share at private four-year colleges also rose slightly, from 16.8% to 17.1%, while the share attending two-year colleges fell from 4.0% to 2.7%.

The small gain in share in the public sector was not evenly distributed across institutional types. The percentage of students attending public universities began the period at 18.1% and rose to 19.1%. The share of students attending public four-year colleges rose more dramatically, from 20.2% to 24.1%. That increase represents about 59,000 more freshmen than would have been enrolled in that sector had the enrollment distribution remained as it was in 1980.[6] By contrast, the share at public two-year colleges fell from 35.8% in 1980 to 31.3% in 1994. This decline means that about 68,000 fewer full-time freshmen were attending community colleges in 1994 than would have been the case had the enrollment distribution been stable over time.[7]

Turning now to the income breakdowns, it is clear that the percentage of students attending private schools in 1994 varies considerably with income. Only 18.5% of lower-income students attended private colleges and universities, a figure that rises to 23.0% for middle-income students and to 53.5% for the richest students. Only 2.6% of all lower-income students enrolled in higher education are at private universities, with 12.8% at private four-year colleges. By contrast, 22.4% of the richest students enrolled in higher education are at private universities, and 27.3% are at private four-year colleges. Middle-income students had intermediate enrollment percentages of 3.9% and 16.6%, respectively. Thus the probability of a student's attending a four-year private college or university depends critically on his or her parents' income.

The chances that a student will attend a public university are generally positively related to parents' income (the exception being the change from the upper-income to the richest income group). The relationship between income and attendance at a public four-year college is more mixed, rising slightly from lower income to upper-middle income and falling for the two more affluent groups.

Perhaps the most striking finding is that 41.0% of upper-income and 47.0% of the richest students attend a university (private or public), compared with only 13.5% of lower-income students. Where do lower-income students disproportionately enroll? Fully 47.3% of lower-income students are at public two-year colleges, almost three and a half times the percentage of upper-income students (13.9%) and five and a half times the percentage of the richest students (8.6%).

How have these proportions changed over time? Comparing 1994 to 1980, the percentage of upper-income students who attend either private or public universities rose from 39.4% to 41.0%, while the percentage of the richest students who attend a university rose from 39.4% to 47.0%. These increases were shared by universities in both the public and the private sectors—contrary to popular belief, the proportion of upper-income students and of the richest students that attend private universities actually *increased* over the period.[8] Rather, it is private four-year colleges that have suffered the loss of affluent students in recent years: the proportion of upper-income students who enrolled at these schools fell from 25.2% to 22.2%, while the proportion of the richest students fell from 31.7% to 27.3%.

That fact undoubtedly accounts for the intense financial pressure that private four-year colleges have appeared to be under over the past decade, as no-need students have become increasingly rare.[9] Interestingly, affluent students have found *public* four-year colleges increasingly attractive, with the proportion attending these schools rising from 15.6% to 20.1% for upper-income students and from 11.9% to 13.3% for the richest students. Middle-income students have similarly increased their share going to public four-year colleges, from 20.4% to 25.2%, with a smaller increase in their share attending public universities (from 17.4% to 18.1%). The share of middle-income students attending private universities was stable (3.9%), while the share attending private four-year colleges increased slightly from 15.8% to 16.6%. The share of lower-income students attending different institutional types generally changed little over time, except for the decline from 5.6% to 3.1% in the share attending two-year private colleges and the increase in the share attending community colleges from 45.9% to 47.3%.

Of all the institutional types, the most striking changes over time were at two-year public colleges. There were considerable changes between 1980 and 1994 in the attractiveness of public two-year colleges to students from different income backgrounds. While the percentage of lower-income students attending community colleges increased over time, the share of students in the other income groups fell dramatically (especially noteworthy are the declines from 38.9% to 33.7% for middle-income students, from 27.6% to 22.1% for upper-middle-income students, and from 14.5% to 8.6% for the richest students). Thus the flight of students from more affluent backgrounds away from public two-year colleges from 1980 to 1994 was in marked contrast to the experience of students from lower-income backgrounds.

These findings raise doubts about some common impressions concerning "middle-income melt." There is no evidence in our data of a

redistribution of middle-income students from either private universities or private four-year colleges. In 1980, some 19.7% of middle-
income students and 24.5% of upper-middle income students were
enrolled at private four-year colleges and universities; fourteen years
later, 20.5% of middle-income students and 25.0% of upper-middle-
income students were in those institutions.

The most striking movement among middle-income students has in
fact been within the public sector, with a sharp decline in the share of
middle-income students at public two-year institutions offset by
growth in the share of middle-income students at public four-year
institutions. Indeed, one of our most interesting findings is the
increase in the representation of low-income students at public two-
year colleges as opposed to the declining representation of middle-
and upper-income students there. It is of course important to remember
that the relatively young, first-time, full-time freshmen represented
in our survey are not the predominant clientele at community colleges. Nonetheless, these data do seem worrisome. They suggest that
the combined effects of tuition increases and limitations on federal
student aid may be impairing the relative ability of lower-income students (relative to their more affluent counterparts) to gain access to
institutions other than community colleges.

A particularly illuminating discovery concerns changes in the representation of students in the upper-income and richest income
brackets at private four-year colleges. Although leaders at these
schools have been vocal in talking about middle-income melt, it appears that what they have experienced is in fact upper-income melt. It
seems likely that this loss of full-pay students is a significant part of
the explanation for the growing interest of these schools in reviewing
their student aid policies and entering into merit aid competition.[10]

These results raise the interesting question of why there hasn't been
middle-income melt in the sense of movement of middle-income students from more to less expensive institutions. These data do not directly address the causes of the patterns we observe. But we can suggest two factors that may be at work. First, many middle-income
students get substantial tuition discounts at private institutions. Increases in discounting may have buffered the effects of a growing
tuition gap. Indeed, as Table 3.5 and Figure 3.1 indicate, more than a
quarter of the tuition increase for middle-income students at private
colleges and universities between 1986–87 and 1992–93 was absorbed
by increased institutional aid. Second, many public colleges and universities have experienced serious budgetary problems, raising
doubts about future quality, imposing obstacles to students' getting
into the classes they need to graduate on time, and so on. These fac-

tors may have tended to push students, including middle-income students, toward private institutions, working to offset middle-income melt.

But what about the finding that high-income students have been leaving private four-year colleges for private and public universities? Again, we can conjecture about possible explanations. Perhaps the phenomenon of "brand-name identification" that became such an important part of American consumerism in the 1980s also took hold in higher education, with students leaving small, usually regional private colleges for larger and better-known universities. This explanation may also help account for the decreased attractiveness of community colleges among middle- and upper-income students.

Stepping back from the details, we find that two broad trends of special importance are revealed in these data. First is the loss of upper-income students at private four-year colleges. This fact goes a long way toward helping us understand the plight of these institutions and their increasingly aggressive marketing and price-discounting policies. Second is the increasing concentration of lower-income students in community colleges. It makes a great deal of sense that as prices rise in public higher education and alternative aid sources fail to keep pace, students of limited means will increasingly find the local community college to be the only viable alternative for postsecondary education. (Table 3.5 and Figure 3.2 indicate that from 1986–87 to 1992–93, the real tuition charges for low-income students at public institutions rose by roughly $1,100. About $300 of that was offset by real aid increases, with the result that net tuition charges rose by $800.) Community colleges may offer excellent opportunities to many young people, but there is no reason why these institutions should be disproportionately attractive to low-income students. The increasing stratification of public higher education by income suggested in these data is a cause for concern.

6

The Future of College Affordability

THE CURRENT situation in American higher education has been shaped by two overarching trends. The first is the rising economic value of education, reflected in the widening earnings gap between those with less and those with more education and resulting in college enrollment rates at or near historic highs. The second is the increasing fiscal squeeze felt by American governments at both the federal and state levels, which has led to governments contributing a declining share of higher education revenues. In one sense, and at least momentarily, this might be seen as the best of both worlds: government's share of higher education costs is lower than it has been since the 1950s, and enrollments are higher than ever.

Yet beneath the surface are signs of a less encouraging reality. Higher net prices for college education have produced a widening gap in enrollments of more and less affluent students. Low-income students are increasingly rare at four-year colleges and universities in both public and private sectors and are heavily concentrated in the community colleges. Meanwhile, four-year private colleges are increasingly starved for high-income, full-pay students and are engaged in price-discounting competitions that threaten to be financially destabilizing.

What is the future likely to hold? It seems likely that the economic returns to education will remain high, as technological developments and an expanding service economy will continue to put a premium on more educated workers. It seems likely as well that the fiscal crisis of American governments will continue. There are no signs of a reversal in Americans' reluctance to pay taxes or of a real willingness by Americans to yield their expectations of substantial government support for medical care, law enforcement, imprisonment, and so on. Caught in that squeeze, it will be hard for lawmakers at either the state or federal level to accord a high priority to spending on higher education.

Against this backdrop, we must consider the echo of the baby boom, which will produce an increase of about one-third in the size of the traditional college-age population over the next decade. With growing demand for places and limited fiscal resources, it seems likely that state institutions will respond by raising tuitions and by increasingly restricting admission to the more prestigious public campuses to students with better academic preparation and therefore, on average, more affluent backgrounds. This trend seems likely to exacerbate the stratification of public higher education by income that we discussed in Chapter 5.

Increasingly restricted state funding is beginning to have another interesting consequence for public colleges and universities. As states come to provide a smaller share of the dollars needed to finance public colleges, their leaders are more and more reluctant to cede control over their activities to state governments. The idea of state universities bargaining for more autonomy from state control in exchange for guaranteed but limited financial support from the state is gaining currency. Presidents calculate that greater freedom to set tuition, revise curriculum, and recruit aggressively may more than make up for a limitation on state funding. The resulting trend toward a sort of semiprivatizing of public colleges may, if it materializes, result in improved quality at some public institutions. It may also, however, reduce the accessibility of these institutions for less affluent students.

All these trends point to the urgency of using increasingly scarce public dollars for higher education well. As we have argued here, recent experience confirms the prediction based on theory and econometric evidence that raising prices for middle- and upper-income students in public higher education will not discourage enrollment. For the same reason, using federal dollars to subsidize the lending costs of middle- and upper-middle-income students is probably not effective in promoting college enrollment.[1] It seems attractive to husband government resources that are now being devoted to subsidies for relatively affluent students and to target them instead on student aid grants for qualified low-income students. The goal should be to provide grants that are adequate to allow qualified low-income students to attend the flagship public university in their home state.

What does the future hold for private colleges and universities? Certainly the expected growth in demand for college enrollment will ease some of the competitive pressures private colleges have been experiencing. Higher prices and tougher admissions standards at public institutions will similarly bolster demand for enrollment at private institutions. Yet not all the trends are positive for the financial health of private institutions. First, the trend toward increasing price competition through student aid discounts and merit aid may prove difficult to reverse even after the decline in demand that touched off the "price war" reverses. The system of need-based financial aid, never as pure as it was sometimes reputed to be, is in pretty bad shape now at many institutions and will be very hard to restore. Second, while demand for private higher education will be bolstered by higher public tuitions, the trend at public colleges toward greater independence from state control may be threatening to some private institutions. A relatively sleepy public university with a large state subsidy and a low tuition may be a less worrisome rival than a higher-priced but more market-oriented publicly assisted institution. Finally, research universities in both public and private sectors face very serious threats to their mission and financial health as Congress contemplates substantial cutbacks in federal research funding.

Are we keeping college affordable? Our review of the evidence relevant to this question puts us in mind of the story of a man who fell from a fortieth-story window. As he fell past the twentieth floor, a colleague leaned out the window and shouted, "Are you OK?" The man hollered back, "So far, so good."

Part Three _____

STUDENT AID AND INSTITUTIONAL STRATEGY

EDUCATIONAL institutions may lack the simple profit motive that economics textbooks attribute to firms, but they nevertheless have interests and respond to incentives. A college or university must, if it is to survive, balance its budget over time; at the same time, institutions and the subgroups that comprise them have interests and aims, and they respond to opportunities and costs when making decisions. In Part Three, we explore the ways that student aid figures into the budgetary situation of colleges and universities and some of the ways in which financial constraints and incentives influence institutional decisions about student aid.

The chapters that follow address issues that have come in for considerable public discussion and controversy. Why have the prices colleges and universities charge risen so rapidly in recent years? To what extent has growth in student tuitions been offset by increases in student aid? Do colleges and universities raise tuition in order to increase the amounts of federally funded student aid they can capture? How are students and families affected by the "bidding wars" that seem to be breaking out among colleges and universities?

The discussion falls into three parts. First, we review the overall revenue and expenditure patterns of American college and universities, focusing on the role of student aid and how that role has changed in recent years. Second, we consider the incentives and opportunities that governmentally financed student aid creates for colleges and universities and present some empirical evidence about institutions' responses to these incentives. This analysis leads to an assessment of current policy proposals, such as the tax credits and deductions for college tuition that President Clinton has proposed, from the standpoint of their impact on state and institutional behavior. Finally, we examine the provision of student aid from the standpoint of individual institutions pursuing their own goals through the use of financial aid as a strategic instrument.

7

Student Aid in Institutional Finance

OVER THE PAST decade or so, there has been a great deal of specula-
tion concerning the course of revenues and expenditures in U.S.
higher education. However, presumably due to data limitations, there
have been few attempts to analyze the recent history of higher education finances at the national level. One exception is our paper (with
Scott W. Blasdell) "Trends in Revenues and Expenditures in U.S.
Higher Education: Where Does the Money Come From? Where Does
It Go?"[1] This chapter updates and expands our earlier work.

First we describe the data set employed in our analysis. Then we
present a detailed look at the recent behavior of higher education
institutions in the nation. We move on to look explicitly at changes
over time in the composition of expenditures and revenues before
summarizing our conclusions.

The Data

Our data set consists of financial and other information on individual
colleges and universities during the period from 1986–87 to 1993–94.
The data come originally from the Integrated Postsecondary Education Data System (IPEDS) administered by the U.S. Department of
Education and describe the basic financial accounts of almost all public and private nonprofit postsecondary institutions in the United
States, along with figures on full- and part-time enrollment for each
institution. The enrollment data allow us to construct estimates of
full-time-equivalent (FTE) enrollment, which we use to express all of
the financial data on a per-FTE-enrollment basis. We have these data
for the majority of private nonprofit and public colleges and universities and concentrate here on three academic years: 1986–87 (referred
to as 1987 in the tables and text that follow), 1990–91 (referred to as
1991), and 1993–94 (referred to as 1994).[2] All of our numbers are adjusted for inflation and are presented in 1993–94 dollars. The data set
has been constructed as a panel so that only schools with data for all
three observation years are included.

In the tables summarizing these data, we disaggregate institutions by Carnegie classification. Table 7.1 presents separate data on expenditures for public and private Research I and II plus Doctorate-Granting I and II universities (referred to here as *research universities*), and Table 7.2 presents analogous data on revenues. Tables 7.3 and 7.4 examine public and private Comprehensive Universities and Colleges I and II (referred to here as *comprehensive universities*). Tables 7.5 and 7.6 consider public and private Liberal Arts Colleges I and II, and Tables 7.7 and 7.8 examine public two-year colleges.[3]

All of our expenditure and revenue categories are explained in detail in the glossary at the end of this chapter. Briefly, expenditure categories include educational and general spending per FTE student net of student aid (NETSPEND),[4] which is then broken down into spending on instruction and self-supported research (INSTRUCT), externally supported research (RESEARCH), public service (PUBSERV), academic support other than library expenditures (ACADSUPP), library expenditures (LIBRARY), student services (STUDSERV), institutional support (INSTSUPP), and operations and maintenance (OPMNEXP).[5] Restricted scholarships (SCLREST), unrestricted scholarships (SCLUNRES), and plant additions (PLANTADD) complete the list of expenditures. Revenue categories include per-FTE values of gross tuition and fees (TANDF), federal grants and contracts (FEDGRCN), state and local grants and contracts (SLGRCN), state and local appropriations (SLAPP), endowment earnings (ENDOWINC),[6] total scholarship aid from institutional funds (TOTSCH), tuition and fee revenue net of institutional aid (NETT&FREV), federal financial aid (FEDFNAID), state and local financial aid (SLFNAID), and the net price paid by the average student (NETSTPR).

A number of these variables are related. Net spending equals the sum of all expenditure variables (plus mandatory and nonmandatory transfers) except for scholarships and plant additions. On the revenue side, gross tuition and fees less scholarship aid from institutional funds equals net tuition and fee revenues, while net tuition and fee revenues less federal and state and local financial aid equals the net student price.

Expenditures and Revenues: Levels and Trends

Table 7.1 shows that net spending per student at private research universities in 1994 was substantially higher than in the public sector ($29,406 versus $15,726, in 1993–94 dollars) and that the difference grew over time (net spending increased at an annual real growth rate of 2.74% at the private schools versus 1.69% in the public sector).

TABLE 7.1
Expenditures at Research and Doctoral Universities (Carnegie Research I and II, Doctoral I and II), 1987–1994 (in 1993–94 dollars)

Expenditure Category	Institution Type*	Expenditure per FTE Student, 1987 ($)	Annual Change, 1987–1991 (%)	Expenditure per FTE Student, 1991 ($)	Annual Change, 1991–1994 (%)	Expenditure per FTE Student, 1994 ($)	Annual Change, 1987–1994 (%)
NETSPEND	Public	13,984	1.82	15,031	1.52	15,726	1.69
	Private	24,332	3.16	27,555	2.19	29,406	2.74
INSTRUCT	Public	5,665	0.71	5,829	0.94	5,996	0.81
	Private	9,619	4.06	11,279	2.60	12,180	3.43
RESEARCH	Public	2,539	5.00	3,087	2.35	3,310	3.86
	Private	4,606	2.32	5,049	1.55	5,287	1.99
PUBSERV	Public	1,035	3.98	1,210	2.05	1,286	3.15
	Private	764	4.18	900	1.55	943	3.05
ACADSUPP	Public	877	1.20	919	3.04	1,006	1.98
	Private	1,566	−0.83	1,514	−0.72	1,482	−0.78

TABLE 7.1 (Continued)

Expenditure Category	Institution Type*	Expenditure per FTE Student, 1987 ($)	Annual Change, 1987–1991 (%)	Expenditure per FTE Student, 1991 ($)	Annual Change, 1991–1994 (%)	Expenditure per FTE Student, 1994 ($)	Annual Change, 1987–1994 (%)
LIBRARY	Public	448	1.46	474	1.96	503	1.68
	Private	793	4.06	930	1.92	985	3.14
STUDSERV	Public	563	1.55	599	2.69	648	2.04
	Private	1,090	3.78	1,265	2.74	1,372	3.33
INSTSUPP	Public	1,199	0.69	1,232	0.54	1,252	0.63
	Private	2,831	2.20	3,088	5.27	3,603	3.50
OPMNEXP	Public	1,235	−1.34	1,170	−0.05	1,168	−0.79
	Private	2,026	1.66	2,164	1.83	2,285	1.74
SCLREST	Public	589	1.57	627	1.53	656	1.55
	Private	1,101	−0.20	1,092	5.56	1,284	2.23
SCLUNRES	Public	251	8.17	344	10.52	464	9.17
	Private	1,488	9.50	2,140	8.31	2,719	8.99
PLANTADD	Public	1,979	6.22	2,519	−8.39	1,937	−0.31
	Private	4,432	−2.25	4,046	2.84	4,401	−0.10
Enrollment	Public	1,416,022	1.60	1,509,012	−0.42	1,490,052	0.73
	Private	467,148	0.98	485,826	0.25	489,464	0.67

*N = 87 public, 58 private.

Although some public-sector expenditures are "off budget" and are therefore not included in these financial data, expenditures per student are strikingly different between sectors, and this difference has been growing over time.[7] In fact, as will be apparent for each of the public-sector groups when we examine them, there has been, at best, only modest real growth after 1987 in net spending per student for students attending public institutions. Private schools, by contrast, have continued to increase net spending at a fairly rapid real rate.

Expenditure growth has varied considerably across spending categories in public higher education. Table 7.1 shows that per-student academic support and student service expenditures have been increasing at an annual real rate of about 2% between 1987 and 1994. Operations and maintenance spending, by contrast, failed to keep pace with inflation, decreasing at an annual real rate of 0.79%. Growth in institutional support and instructional expenditures was in between, rising at annual rates of 0.63% and 0.81%, respectively.[8] Turning to private research universities, real growth in most categories is considerable (over 3% for library, student services, and institutional support) and far exceeds that in the public sector. The exception is academic support, where per-student expenditures at private research universities have been declining over the period. The differences in growth rates between the private and public institutions imply that the already substantial disparities in levels of particular expenditures have tended to increase further over time. For example, in 1987, institutional support expenditures per FTE student at private research universities amounted to $2,831, versus $1,199 at their public counterparts. With an annual real growth rate of 3.5%, spending at private universities rose by $772 by 1994, while the annual growth rate of 0.63% resulted in an increase of only $53 at public universities. As a result, the difference in per-student spending increased from $1,632 to $2,351 over the seven-year period.

However, annual growth rates in spending in all of these categories are drawfed by the increases in scholarships from unrestricted funds. While both private and public research universities have increased spending by a staggering annual real rate of about 9%, the much higher starting point for private schools has resulted in a substantially greater absolute increase. We return to the financial aid question when we discuss revenues.

Whereas all but the final expenditure category in the table relates to the operating budget, the last category, plant additions, relates to the capital budget. In our earlier paper, we showed that private institutions were engaged in a massive building boom in the 1980s. In 1979, per-student additions to plant and equipment were almost identical in the public and private sectors, but over the subsequent decade, plant additions grew to be twice as large on a per-student basis at private universities as at public universities. However, our latest data show that the difference in spending stopped growing after 1987 as private research universities ended their building boom. Between 1987 and 1991, per-student capital expenditures at private research universities fell in real terms by 2.25% per year. Though growth was restored after 1991, the total change over the 1987–1994 period was slightly negative. Public research universities experienced a rapid increase in building between 1987 and 1991 but an even more rapid decline in plant additions after 1991. The turnaround in 1991 is not at all surprising given the striking decline in state and local appropriations for public schools that occurred at that time (this will be discussed shortly).

Table 7.2 shows that although gross tuition and fees (the sticker price) are far greater at private research universities than at their public counterparts ($14,963 versus $3,963), annual real growth rates over the entire period were higher in the public sector (4.35%) than in the private sector (3.38%). This is the result of changes in the public sector in recent years: private tuition rose at a fairly constant annual real rate of around 3.4% during the two subperiods, while public tuition increases jumped from 2.9% to 6.3%.

Moving down the list of revenue categories, the reason for stringency in public-sector expenditures quickly becomes apparent: state and local appropriations failed to keep pace with inflation (with an annual real decline of 0.86%). Interestingly, although the largest annual declines in this key revenue source occurred after 1991 (the annual real decline between 1991 and 1994 was 1.54%), problems in the public sector started earlier, as evidenced by an annual per-student decline in state and local appropriations of 0.35% between 1987 and 1991. State and local appropriations are by far the major revenue source for public institutions ($6,815 accounts for 43% of the $15,726 net spending figure), and the real decline over the seven-year period is the obvious cause of the modest growth (or decline) in the various expenditure categories.

Universities in both sectors have increased institutional financial aid at spectacular real rates—TOTSCH increased at an annual rate of 9.72% in the public sector and 8.37% in the private sector over the entire period.[9] A breakdown by subperiods indicates that the rate of increase in private expenditures on financial aid is slackening a bit (7.92% annual real growth between 1991 and 1994 versus 8.71% between 1987 and 1991) but that the growth path remains extremely steep.

TABLE 7.2
Revenues of Research and Doctoral Universities (Carnegie Research I and II, Doctoral I and II), 1987–1994 (in 1993–94 dollars)

Revenue Category	Institution Type*	Revenue per FTE Student, 1987 ($)	Annual Change, 1987–1991 (%)	Revenue per FTE Student, 1991 ($)	Annual Change, 1991–1994 (%)	Revenue per FTE Student, 1994 ($)	Annual Change, 1987–1994 (%)
TANDF	Public	2,942	2.91	3,300	6.30	3,963	4.35
	Private	11,853	3.31	13,501	3.49	14,963	3.38
FEDGRCN	Public	1,911	3.97	2,233	4.69	2,562	4.27
	Private	5,138	1.95	5,550	1.55	5,813	1.78
SLGRCN	Public	329	7.36	438	2.15	467	5.09
	Private	673	2.96	756	3.20	831	3.06
SLAPP	Public	7,242	−0.35	7,141	−1.54	6,815	−0.86
	Private	301	−3.37	263	−11.19	184	−6.80
ENDOWINC	Public	154	1.97	166	10.72	225	5.63
	Private	2,143	3.27	2,437	4.17	2,754	3.65
TOTSCH	Public	208	8.77	291	11.00	397	9.72
	Private	1,760	8.71	2,458	7.92	3,089	8.37

TABLE 7.2 (Continued)

Revenue Category	Institution Type*	Revenue per FTE Student, 1987 ($)	Annual Change, 1987–1991 (%)	Revenue per FTE Student, 1991 ($)	Annual Change, 1991–1994 (%)	Revenue per FTE Student, 1994 ($)	Annual Change, 1987–1994 (%)
NETT&FREV	Public	2,734	2.42	3,009	5.82	3,566	3.87
	Private	10,093	2.27	11,043	2.45	11,874	2.35
FEDFNAID	Public	390	1.46	413	0.03	414	0.84
	Private	424	0.34	430	5.96	512	2.71
SLFNAID	Public	129	2.65	143	9.75	190	5.63
	Private	106	−5.68	84	15.48	129	2.87
NETSTPR	Public	2,215	2.58	2,452	6.51	2,963	4.24
	Private	9,563	2.44	10,530	2.18	11,234	2.33
Enrollment	Public	1,416,022	1.60	1,509,012	−0.42	1,490,052	0.73
	Private	467,148	0.98	485,826	0.25	489,464	0.67

*N = 87 public, 58 private.

The rapid increase in financial aid means that net tuition and fee revenues have increased less rapidly than gross tuition. The largest differences occur for the private universities, with sticker prices increasing at an annual real rate of almost 3.5% while tuition revenues are increasing by less than 2.5%. This important point—that large increases in gross tuition have been resulting in substantially smaller increases in actual revenues—motivates much of the behavior discussed in other chapters (the more strategic allocation of tuition discounts, the increase in merit aid, and so on). Finally, increases in financial aid provided by the government (federal, state, and local) have failed to soften the blow of rapid increases in sticker prices at public research universities, the bottom line being an annual real increase in price for an average student of 4.24%, roughly equivalent to the increase in gross tuition at those schools. The annual real increase in the price for a student attending a private research university is considerably lower (2.33%), resulting much more from increases in institutional aid than from increases in financial aid from the government.

Tables 7.3 and 7.4 provide expenditure and revenue data for comprehensive universities. As Table 7.3 shows, although the private-public difference in net spending per student ($10,917 versus $8,460) is much smaller than was the case for research universities, the annual growth rate differential (1.45% for private comprehensive universities and 0.46% for public universities) implies some widening over time. Declines in real expenditures at public schools in instruction (0.08% annually) plus small real growth rates in library expenditures (0.77%) and student services (1.60%) can be contrasted with growth rates at private comprehensive universities of 1.44%, 3.57%, and 3.26%, respectively. Even in the case of operations and maintenance, where spending at private comprehensive universities has failed to keep pace with inflation, these schools came closer (an annual real decline of 0.22%) than public comprehensives (an annual real decline of 2.18%). Again, there was striking growth in financial aid from unrestricted funds at private schools, and plant additions fell in the public sector after 1991.

Table 7.4 shows that growth rates in gross tuition and fees, institutional financial aid, net tuition and fees, and the net price for students mirrored fairly closely the experience of research universities. Again, substantial increases in financial aid led to the situation where net tuition revenues increased more slowly than sticker prices, especially in the private sector, where sticker prices increased at a real annual rate of 3.71% while net tuition revenues rose at a rate of 2.64%. Finally, there was a considerable drop in state and local appropriations for public comprehensive universities, showing an annual rate of

TABLE 7.3
Expenditures at Comprehensive Universities (Carnegie Comprehensive I and II), 1987–1994 (in 1993–94 dollars)

Expenditure Category	Institution Type*	Expenditure per FTE Student, 1987 ($)	Annual Change, 1987–1991 (%)	Expenditure per FTE Student, 1991 ($)	Annual Change, 1991–1994 (%)	Expenditure per FTE Student, 1994 ($)	Annual Change, 1987–1994 (%)
NETSPEND	Public	8,192	−0.14	8,148	1.26	8,460	0.46
	Private	9,868	1.01	10,272	2.05	10,917	1.45
INSTRUCT	Public	3,886	−0.32	3,836	0.25	3,865	−0.08
	Private	4,077	1.32	4,296	1.60	4,506	1.44
RESEARCH	Public	229	0.38	233	1.21	241	0.73
	Private	126	3.54	145	27.35	299	13.15
PUBSERV	Public	252	2.75	281	6.63	340	4.40
	Private	170	−1.45	160	4.17	181	0.92
ACADSUPP	Public	483	1.00	502	1.29	522	1.12
	Private	547	0.11	550	0.85	564	0.43

LIBRARY	Public	302	1.10	315	0.33	318	0.77
	Private	298	5.30	366	1.31	381	3.57
STUDSERV	Public	614	1.83	660	1.29	686	1.60
	Private	1,043	3.57	1,200	2.84	1,305	3.26
INSTSUPP	Public	1,105	−0.01	1,104	0.30	1,114	0.12
	Private	1,933	0.72	1,989	0.06	1,992	0.43
OPMNEXP	Public	1,034	−3.03	914	−1.03	887	−2.18
	Private	1,064	−0.91	1,025	0.70	1,047	−0.22
SCLREST	Public	720	1.26	757	2.33	811	1.72
	Private	814	3.96	950	3.84	1,064	3.91
SCLUNRES	Public	162	4.63	194	7.91	244	6.03
	Private	932	7.95	1,265	12.57	1,805	9.91
PLANTADD	Public	1,081	1.56	1,151	−6.08	953	−1.79
	Private	1,224	5.11	1,494	0.06	1,497	2.91
Enrollment	Public	941,191	3.25	1,069,737	1.26	1,110,633	2.39
	Private	340,468	2.78	379,899	1.55	397,820	2.25

*N = 170 public, 153 private.

TABLE 7.4
Revenues of Comprehensive Universities (Carnegie Comprehensive I and II), 1987–1994 (in 1993–94 dollars)

Revenue Category	Institution Type*	Revenue per FTE Student, 1987 ($)	Annual Change, 1987–1991 (%)	Revenue per FTE Student, 1991 ($)	Annual Change, 1991–1994 (%)	Revenue per FTE Student, 1994 ($)	Annual Change, 1987–1994 (%)
TANDF	Public	2,066	3.23	2,347	6.93	2,869	4.80
	Private	7,704	3.54	8,855	3.93	9,940	3.71
FEDGRCN	Public	384	-0.28	379	7.68	474	3.06
	Private	292	2.97	328	12.43	466	6.93
SLGRCN	Public	199	3.93	233	7.29	287	5.36
	Private	234	8.06	319	8.95	412	8.44
SLAPP	Public	5,463	-2.51	4,936	-2.90	4,518	-2.68
	Private	100	-0.65	97	-12.32	65	-5.83
ENDOWINC	Public	0		0		0	
	Private	374	3.00	421	5.89	500	4.23

TOTSCH	Public	116	9.07	165	8.11	208	8.66
	Private	1,016	7.62	1,363	11.99	1,915	9.47
NETT&FREV	Public	1,950	2.85	2,182	6.84	2,661	4.54
	Private	6,688	2.88	7,492	2.32	8,025	2.64
FEDFNAID	Public	611	0.41	621	−0.35	615	0.08
	Private	462	2.16	503	0.65	513	1.51
SLFNAID	Public	124	1.00	129	14.78	194	6.69
	Private	168	8.17	229	11.16	315	9.44
NETSTPR	Public	1,215	4.19	1,432	8.94	1,852	6.20
	Private	6,059	2.77	6,760	2.11	7,197	2.49
Enrollment	Public	941,191	3.25	1,069,737	1.26	1,110,633	2.39
	Private	340,468	2.78	379,899	1.55	397,820	2.25

*N = 170 public, 153 private.

decline of 2.51% from 1987 to 1991 and 2.90% from 1991 to 1994. Not only is the decline greater for this group of schools than for public research universities, but state and local appropriations in 1994 accounted for 53% of net spending at public comprehensive universities ($4,518 out of $8,460), compared with 43% in the earlier case.

Tables 7.5 and 7.6 present information for liberal arts colleges. As Table 7.5 shows, private liberal arts colleges have experienced real growth in net spending over the 1987–1994 period (1.76% per year) that is between the growth rates at private research universities (2.74%) and private comprehensives (1.45%). Again, there was rapid real growth in financial aid (an annual growth rate of 9.68% in scholarships from unrestricted funds) and considerable real increases in spending in various categories (such as the 2.38%, 3.46%, and 2.84% growth rates for academic support, library, and student services, respectively). Though capital expenditures fell after 1991, the decline (3.64% per year) was much less dramatic than at public liberal arts colleges (14.32%). On the revenue side, we again see, in Table 7.6, the familiar pattern of financial aid increases wiping out a good portion of the increase in gross tuition in the private sector—while private liberal arts colleges increased sticker prices at an annual real rate of 3.82% throughout this period, tuition revenues increased at a rate of only 2.27%. Caution is suggested by the relatively small sample size for public liberal arts colleges (forty-four institutions enrolling around 113,000 FTE students), but the data mirror pretty closely the experience of public comprehensive universities, especially on the revenue side.

Tables 7.7 and 7.8 examine our final institutional category, community colleges. These schools have experienced a small annual real decline in net spending (0.18%) over the period and have even managed to keep instructional expenditures flat despite a real decline in state and local appropriations of 1.62% per year. One reason for this is that institutional financial aid is so small that increases in gross tuition (4.29% annually) translate almost directly into increases in net tuition revenue (4.13% annually). However, the increase in government financial aid has lessened the blow to students attending community colleges, whose costs have been increasing at an annual real rate of 1.46%, far below the rise in sticker prices.

Expenditures and Revenues: Changes in Composition

Tables 7.9 and 7.10 present the expenditure and revenue data in a different manner. Table 7.9 shows the share of net spending going to

TABLE 7.5
Expenditures at Liberal Arts Colleges (Carnegie Liberal Arts I and II), 1987–1994 (in 1993–94 dollars)

Expenditure Category	Institution Type*	Expenditure per FTE Student, 1987 ($)	Annual Change, 1987–1991 (%)	Expenditure per FTE Student, 1991 ($)	Annual Change, 1991–1994 (%)	Expenditure per FTE Student, 1994 ($)	Annual Change, 1987–1994 (%)
NETSPEND	Public	7,559	-0.32	7,463	0.08	7,481	-0.15
	Private	11,086	1.95	11,976	1.50	12,524	1.76
INSTRUCT	Public	3,446	-0.33	3,401	-0.88	3,312	-0.57
	Private	4,162	2.14	4,529	1.60	4,749	1.90
RESEARCH	Public	42	21.33	92	6.45	111	14.71
	Private	84	0.59	86	12.28	122	5.44
PUBSERV	Public	235	6.51	302	3.32	333	5.13
	Private	98	1.29	103	2.05	109	1.61
ACADSUPP	Public	464	-2.50	419	3.41	463	-0.01
	Private	512	2.40	563	2.36	604	2.38
LIBRARY	Public	275	3.75	319	-4.79	275	0.00
	Private	405	4.44	482	2.17	514	3.46
STUDSERV	Public	654	0.81	675	-0.41	667	0.28
	Private	1,406	3.66	1,623	1.76	1,710	2.84

TABLE 7.5 (Continued)

Expenditure Category	Institution Type*	Expenditure per FTE Student, 1987 ($)	Annual Change, 1987–1991 (%)	Expenditure per FTE Student, 1991 ($)	Annual Change, 1991–1994 (%)	Expenditure per FTE Student, 1994 ($)	Annual Change, 1987–1994 (%)
INSTSUPP	Public	1,202	−0.60	1,174	−1.78	1,112	−1.11
	Private	2,448	1.06	2,553	1.02	2,632	1.04
OPMNEXP	Public	1,067	−3.42	928	−2.65	856	−3.09
	Private	1,410	0.26	1,425	−0.66	1,397	−0.13
SCLREST	Public	902	2.77	1,007	2.04	1,070	2.46
	Private	1,310	3.00	1,474	2.80	1,602	2.92
SCLUNRES	Public	107	6.72	139	6.45	168	6.61
	Private	1,330	8.17	1,821	11.73	2,540	9.68
PLANTADD	Public	1,155	1.60	1,231	−14.32	774	−5.56
	Private	1,813	6.04	2,293	−3.64	2,051	1.78
Enrollment	Public	88,246	4.05	103,440	2.92	112,780	3.57
	Private	326,431	2.29	357,336	1.38	372,351	1.90

*N = 44 public, 283 private.

TABLE 7.6
Revenues of Liberal Arts Colleges (Carnegie Liberal Arts I and II), 1987–1994 (in 1993–94 dollars)

Revenue Category	Institution Type*	Revenue per FTE Student, 1987 ($)	Annual Change, 1987–1991 (%)	Revenue per FTE Student, 1991 ($)	Annual Change, 1991–1994 (%)	Revenue per FTE Student, 1994 ($)	Annual Change, 1987–1994 (%)
TANDF	Public	1,841	2.86	2,060	7.40	2,552	4.78
	Private	8,328	3.93	9,718	3.66	10,823	3.82
FEDGRCN	Public	310	1.76	332	5.18	386	3.21
	Private	232	0.41	236	5.57	278	2.59
SLGRCN	Public	199	6.64	257	12.70	368	9.20
	Private	281	11.08	428	4.95	495	8.41
SLAPP	Public	5,108	−2.18	4,678	−4.16	4,118	−3.03
	Private	90	−4.86	74	−19.21	39	−11.30
ENDOWINC	Public	0		0		0	
	Private	1,164	3.39	1,330	8.16	1,683	5.41
TOTSCH	Public	85	11.15	129	5.87	154	8.85
	Private	1,540	8.21	2,111	10.93	2,882	9.37

TABLE 7.6 (Continued)

Revenue Category	Institution Type*	Revenue per FTE Student, 1987 ($)	Annual Change, 1987–1991 (%)	Revenue per FTE Student, 1991 ($)	Annual Change, 1991–1994 (%)	Revenue per FTE Student, 1994 ($)	Annual Change, 1987–1994 (%)
NETT&FREV	Public	1,756	2.41	1,931	7.50	2,399	4.56
	Private	6,788	2.89	7,607	1.44	7,941	2.27
FEDFNAID	Public	743	1.96	803	−0.66	787	0.83
	Private	668	−0.71	649	0.13	652	−0.35
SLFNAID	Public	142	−0.21	140	19.63	240	7.86
	Private	252	8.06	343	6.12	410	7.23
NETSTPR	Public	871	3.18	987	11.56	1,371	6.69
	Private	5,869	3.04	6,615	1.32	6,880	2.30
Enrollment	Public	88,246	4.05	103,440	2.92	112,780	3.57
	Private	326,431	2.29	357,336	1.38	372,351	1.90

*N = 44 public, 283 private.

TABLE 7.7
Expenditures at Community Colleges (Public Carnegie Two-Year Schools),* 1987–1994
in 1993–94 dollars)

Expenditure Category	Expenditure per FTE Student, 1987 ($)	Annual Change, 1987–1991 (%)	Expenditure per FTE Student, 1991 ($)	Annual Change, 1991–1994 (%)	Expenditure per FTE Student, 1994 ($)	Annual Change, 1987–1994 (%)
NETSPEND	6,349	−0.09	6,327	−0.31	6,268	−0.18
INSTRUCT	3,174	0.17	3,196	−0.14	3,182	0.03
RESEARCH	4	11.19	6	22.44	11	15.88
PUBSERV	133	3.14	150	−0.88	146	1.40
ACADSUPP	411	−1.49	387	−0.42	382	−1.03
LIBRARY	164	1.32	173	−1.54	165	0.08
STUDSERV	586	0.46	597	2.04	635	1.14
INSTSUPP	1,029	−0.07	1,027	−1.69	976	−0.76
OPMNEXP	722	−1.60	676	−0.92	658	−1.31
CLREST	515	4.83	623	9.40	815	6.77
CLUNRES	41	2.73	45	11.76	63	6.51
PLANTADD	688	4.43	818	−3.37	738	1.02
Enrollment	1,084,888	3.61	1,250,309	3.06	1,368,767	3.38

*N = 393.

each expenditure category in 1987 and 1994 for each type of institution.[10]

Starting with the 1987 figures, the dominant category for all groups is instruction and self-supported research, accounting for roughly 40% to 50% of operating expenditures. Whereas academic support,

TABLE 7.8
Revenues of Community Colleges (Public Carnegie Two-Year Schools),* 1987–1994
in 1993–94 dollars)

Revenue Category	Revenue per FTE Student, 1987 ($)	Annual Change, 1987–1991 (%)	Revenue per FTE Student, 1991 ($)	Annual Change, 1991–1994 (%)	Revenue per FTE Student, 1994 ($)	Annual Change, 1987–1994 (%)
FUNDF	1,108	2.98	1,246	6.07	1,487	4.29
EDGRCN	280	−1.56	263	10.43	354	3.41
LGRCN	245	2.28	268	3.83	301	2.94
LAPP	4,611	−1.08	4,415	−2.32	4,114	−1.62
NDOWINC	0		0		0	
OTSCH	40	6.08	50	11.19	69	8.24
NETT&FREV	1,068	2.86	1,195	5.85	1,417	4.13
EDFNAID	447	5.04	544	7.85	682	6.24
LFNAID	55	0.14	55	25.19	108	10.19
NETSTPR	566	1.30	596	1.68	627	1.46
Enrollment	1,084,888	3.61	1,250,309	3.06	1,368,767	3.38

*N = 393.

TABLE 7.9
Breakdown of Expenditures, 1987 and 1994 (%)

	Research and Doctoral		Comprehensive		Liberal Arts		Two-Ye
	Public	Private	Public	Private	Public	Private	Publi
1987							
Instruction and self-							
supported research	41.77	41.29	49.16	44.04	46.66	39.54	51.00
Funded research	18.72	19.77	2.90	1.36	0.57	0.80	0.06
Public service	7.63	3.28	3.19	1.84	3.18	0.93	2.14
Academic support	6.47	6.72	6.11	5.91	6.28	4.86	6.60
Library	3.30	3.40	3.82	3.22	3.72	3.85	2.64
Student services	4.15	4.68	7.77	11.27	8.86	13.36	9.42
Institutional support	8.84	12.15	13.98	20.88	16.28	23.26	16.54
Operations and							
maintenance	9.11	8.70	13.08	11.49	14.45	13.40	11.60
1994							
Instruction and self-							
supported research	39.53	43.29	48.48	43.85	46.46	40.12	51.70
Funded research	21.82	18.79	3.02	2.91	1.56	1.03	0.18
Public service	8.48	3.35	4.26	1.76	4.67	0.92	2.37
Academic support	6.63	5.27	6.55	5.49	6.49	5.10	6.21
Library	3.32	3.50	3.99	3.71	3.86	4.34	2.68
Student services	4.27	4.88	8.60	12.70	9.36	14.45	10.32
Institutional support	8.25	12.81	13.97	19.39	15.60	22.24	15.86
Operations and							
maintenance	7.70	8.12	11.13	10.19	12.01	11.80	10.69

library expenditures, and operations and maintenance account for a fairly consistent percentage of expenditures (5 to 7%, 3 to 4% and 9 to 14%, respectively), there is much greater variation across institutional types for the other expenditure groups. Differences in the role of funded research and public service are to be expected, but there is also a good deal of variation in relative spending on student services and institutional support. Specifically, private schools allocate a greater percentage of operating expenditures to student services and institutional support than their public counterparts do—17% total versus 13% for research universities, 32% versus 22% for comprehensive universities, and 37% versus 25% for liberal arts colleges.

Looking at changes over time in expenditure shares, there is a great deal of stability from 1987 to 1994, although it is interesting to note that by the end of the period, one expenditure category, operations

TABLE 7.10
Breakdown of Revenues, 1987 and 1994 (%)

	Research and Doctoral		Comprehensive		Liberal Arts		Two-Year
	Public	Private	Public	Private	Public	Private	Public
1987							
Federal grants and contracts	15.45	28.00	4.80	3.80	4.20	2.71	4.51
State and local grants and contracts	2.66	3.67	2.49	3.04	2.69	3.29	3.95
State and local appropriations	58.54	1.64	68.32	1.30	69.29	1.05	74.32
Endowment income	1.24	11.68	0.00	4.87	0.00	13.61	0.00
Net tuition revenue	22.10	55.01	24.39	87.00	23.82	79.34	17.21
1994							
Federal grants and contracts	18.79	27.09	5.96	4.92	5.31	2.66	5.73
State and local grants and contracts	3.42	3.87	3.62	4.35	5.06	4.74	4.86
State and local appropriations	49.98	0.86	56.90	0.69	56.64	0.37	66.50
Endowment income	1.65	12.84	0.00	5.28	0.00	16.13	0.00
Net tuition revenue	26.15	55.34	33.51	84.75	32.99	76.09	22.91

and maintenance, accounted for a smaller share of operating expenditures for each institutional group.

The numbers in Table 7.10 examine the percentage contribution of each of our major revenue sources.[11] In 1994, private schools received most of their revenues from tuition, ranging from 55% at research universities to 85% at comprehensive universities, with liberal arts colleges at 76%. The major funding source in the public sector is state and local appropriations, which account for 67% of revenues at community colleges, 50% of revenues at research universities, and 57% at other public colleges and universities. Other significant revenue sources are federal grants and contracts at public and private research universities (accounting for 19% and 27% of revenues, respectively), endowment income at private research universities and liberal arts colleges (accounting for 13% and 16% of revenues), and net tuition revenue at public research universities (26% of revenues), public comprehensive universities (34% of revenues), public liberal arts colleges (33% of revenues), and community colleges (23%).

In terms of changes in revenue shares over time, the most striking

movement is in the relative contribution from the government as opposed to students at public institutions. For all four public institutional groups, the share of revenues contributed by state and local
appropriations has declined—from 59% to 50% at research universities, from 68% to 57% at comprehensives, from 69% to 57% at liberal
arts colleges, and from 74% to 67% at community colleges—while the
share of revenues contributed by net tuition revenue has increased—
from 22% to 26%, 24% to 34%, 24% to 33%, and 17% to 23%, respectively. Although tuition dependence in the public sector remains
much less than among private colleges and universities, the experience during the 1987–1994 period suggests that the narrowing trend
noted in our earlier work has accelerated.[12]

Conclusion

The aim of this chapter was to use the latest national data available to
address two key questions concerning American higher education:
Where does the money come from? And where does it go? Of particular importance is how changes in sticker prices have translated into
changes in net tuition revenues and in the prices students must pay.
Recognizing the heterogeneity of institutions of higher education in
the United States, we have asked these questions for a variety of institutional types.

On the expenditure side, financial problems have tended to take
their toll on certain expenditure categories—most notably operations
and maintenance—rather than leading to across-the-board reductions. Such behavior suggests an intergenerational cost transfer, with
increasingly scarce resources being more likely to be spent on current
students, faculty, and staff (in the form of instructional spending and
self-supported research, among other expenditure categories) rather
than on future generations. One very clear difference between these
findings and our earlier ones is that the deterioration in the financial
climate in recent years has put an end to the boom in capital spending that we had previously documented. Again, this is consistent with
allocating resources more to the present than to the future.

The reason for financial problems for public institutions is their dis-
mal experience with their principal revenue source, state and local
appropriations. Real declines in these appropriations, particularly after 1991, have forced public schools of all types to become more tu-
ition-dependent. The failure of financial aid (federal, state, local, or
institutional) to keep pace with the increases in gross tuition means
that, from 1991 to 1994, students attending public colleges and univer-

sities have had the average real net price they pay increase by 2% to 12% per year above inflation. The worry about this trend is whether needy students are being "held harmless"—whether increases in public tuition are being targeted on those students who can afford to pay. The results presented elsewhere in this book indicate that they are not. This has endangered the progress we have made over the past three decades in terms of access and choice in higher education for low-income students.

The biggest difficulty private colleges and universities face relates to institutional financial aid. Real annual growth rates for different groups of private schools have ranged from 8% to 9% from 1987 to 1991 and from 8% to 12% during the 1991–1994 period. A natural temptation would be to increase private gross tuition at rapid rates in recognition of the fact that a substantial portion of gross revenues will be recycled in financial aid. However, an alternative perspective suggests that rapid increases in gross tuition generate increasingly little in terms of actual revenues, making large tuition hikes not worth the political fallout. What is clear is that a considerable gap has developed between the course of gross tuition changes and net tuition revenues, inducing schools to place their tuition and financial aid policies under intense scrutiny.

Glossary of Expenditure and Revenue Categories

Expenditures

Netspend — net spending per FTE student. We compute this number as the average per-FTE-student value of educational and general spending net of student aid. We have netted out student aid spending because part of this spending is directly "passed through" from federal student aid, and for most schools the rest is best seen as forgone institutional revenue, rather than as spending on educational programs.

Instruct — instruction and self-supported research per FTE student. Expenditures of the colleges, schools, departments, and other instructional divisions of the institution and expenditures for departmental research and public service that are not separately budgeted are included. Expenditures for academic administration where the primary function is administration (e.g., academic deans) are excluded.

Research — research per FTE student. All funds expended for activities specifically organized to produce research outcomes and either commissioned by an agency external to the institution or separately budgeted by an organizational unit within the institution are included.

Pubserv — public service per FTE student. This category includes all funds budgeted specifically for public service and expended for activities established primarily to provide noninstructional services beneficial to groups external to the institution. Examples are seminars and projects provided to particular sectors of the community, community services, and cooperative extension projects.

Acadsupp — academic support per FTE student. Expenditures for the support services that are an integral part of the institution's primary missions of instruction, research, or public service are included. Expenditures for museums, galleries, audiovisual services, academic computing support, ancillary support, academic administration, personnel development, and course and curriculum development are examples. We have taken out library expenditures and treated them as a separate category.

Library — library spending per FTE student. Expenditures on library materials.

Studserv — student services per FTE student. This category includes funds expended for admissions, registrar activities, and activities whose primary purpose is to contribute to students' emotional and physical well-being and to their intellectual, cultural, and social development outside the context of the formal instruction program. Examples are career guidance, counseling, financial aid administration, student health services (except when operated as a self-supporting auxiliary enterprise), and the administrative allowance for Pell grants.

Instsupp — institutional support per FTE student. Included are expenditures for the day-to-day operational support of the institution, excluding expenditures for physical plant operations. Examples are general administrative services, executive direction and planning, legal and fiscal operations, and community relations.

Opmnexp — operations and maintenance per FTE student. This category includes all expenditures for operations established to provide service and maintenance related to campus grounds and facilities used for educational and general purposes. Expenditures made from institutional plant funds accounts are excluded.

Sclrest — scholarships from restricted funds per FTE student. Included are scholarships and fellowships awarded from restricted funds, including Pell grants.

Sclunres — scholarships from unrestricted funds per FTE student. Included are scholarships and fellowships awarded from unrestricted funds. This category, as well as SCLREST, applies only to funds given in the form of outright grants and trainee stipends to individuals enrolled in formal coursework, either for credit or not. Aid to students in the form of tuition or fee remissions are included (except remissions granted because of faculty or staff status). College work-study program expenses are reported where the student served, not in either of the scholarship categories.

Plantadd — plant additions per FTE student. We compute this number by summing over the three categories of physical plant additions during the year—land, buildings, and equipment. Additions during the year are purchases, in-kind gifts from donors, and other additions to plant. Construction in progress and plant expenditures that represent capital fund investments in real estate are excluded.

Revenues

Tandf — gross tuition and fee revenue per FTE student. The convention followed by academic institutions is to calculate this amount by assuming that every student pays the sticker or list price; hence this variable is gross of financial aid. Charges for room, board, and other services rendered by auxiliary enterprises are excluded.

Fedgrcn — federal grants and contracts per FTE student less Pell and SEOG amounts. Examples are research projects, training programs, and similar activities for which amounts are received or expenditures are reimbursable under the terms of a government grant or contract.

Slgrcn — state and local grants and contracts per FTE student.

Slapp — state and local appropriations per FTE student. This category includes all amounts received or made available to an institution through acts of a legislative body, except grants of contracts. These funds are for meeting current operating expenses and not for specific projects or programs.

Endowinc — endowment income per FTE student. We compute this by taking 5% of the market value of the endowment at the beginning of the academic year. The 5% figure is a proxy for the average availment rate used by colleges and universities. Although the Integrated Postsecondary Education Data System (IPEDS) form asks directly for endowment income, respondents are asked to reply on the basis of the particular availment formula they use. For some, the answer will be based on total return, but for others, the answer will be based only on yield. We therefore use our 5% method as the best proxy we can find for endowment income. Endowment figures for many community colleges, public liberal arts colleges, and public comprehensive universities were lacking, and for institutions reporting a figure, it was almost always extremely small. We therefore set ENDOWINC to zero for all public schools other than public research universities.

Totsch — total scholarship aid from institutional funds per FTE student.

Nett&frev — net tuition and fee revenue per FTE student. We subtract the total amount of scholarship aid from institutional funds (TOTSCH) from gross tuition and fees (TANDF) to calculate this net revenue figure.

Fedfnaid — the sum of Pell and SEOG grants disbursed per FTE student. Administrative expenses are included for SEOG.

Slfnaid — state and local financial aid per FTE student.

Netstpr — net student price. This figure is calculated by taking gross tuition and subtracting institutional aid, federal aid, and state and local aid.

8

How Government Aid Shapes Colleges' Behavior

As MADE CLEAR in Chapter 7, student aid is a financially significant item for most colleges and universities. Particularly in these times of tight competition and heavy financial pressure on institutions, colleges and universities are bound to attend closely to the management of aid dollars. It would be naive to suppose that academic managers would neglect the incentives created, consciously or otherwise, by external programs that affect student financing of college. If, for example, a federal student aid program is designed so that colleges can easily capture additional aid dollars by raising their prices, it is reasonable to expect schools to do it.

These issues became a matter of intense debate in the mid-1980s when then Secretary of Education William Bennett advanced the claim that increases in federal student aid were an important cause of tuition inflation (Bennett 1987). Recently, President Clinton's proposals for tax cuts for college tuition have rekindled the debate. Critics have worried that tax credits or tax deductions for college tuition will, on one hand, make it easier for colleges to boost tuition and, on the other hand, allow colleges and state governments to reduce their own aid commitments as federal tax rebates take up the slack.

Unfortunately, the quality of the analysis of such potential incentive effects in the literature on pricing and student aid often disappoints. Some critics of higher education—former Secretary Bennett included—have made bold claims in this area without pausing to develop either the detailed arguments or the empirical evidence that would lend credibility to the claims. The frequent repetition of such claims is sometimes confused with evidence for them. Yet much analysis of and policy work on higher education proceeds as if such incentive effects could be safely neglected, operating as if universities, colleges, and state governments set their pricing and aid policies with no attention to the impact that external funding has on their decisions.

To do better is not easy. The impact of incentive effects on a nonprofit or state-run institution should not casually be assumed to be identical to the impact of the same incentive on a profit-maximizing institution. Yet we have no theory of the conduct of nonprofit institutions that is as well thought out or successful as theories based on the assumption of profit maximization have been in some areas of economics. Moreover, data to investigate such incentive effects are hard to come by and, in the absence of a well-supported theoretical model, hard to interpret.

This chapter has two principal aims. First, we attempt to bring the best available theoretical and empirical analysis to bear on the underlying questions. Second, we discuss in some detail issues surrounding the potential incentive effects of policy alternatives that are under active discussion in Washington, including tax preferences for college tuition and substantial increases in the size of Pell grants. We comment on the likely nature and significance of such incentive effects and also attempt to clarify the question of what sorts of incentive effects might be judged desirable and undesirable.

Theory and Evidence

It is useful to begin our analysis by considering William Bennett's forceful claim that federal student aid increases have backfired by causing private colleges to raise tuition to capture the additional aid, with the result that aid goes mainly to benefit college revenues rather than to ease the payment burden for students. The argument for this assertion often goes no further than to cite the analogy to medical care. Under the payment systems that prevailed in federal medical insurance until recently, a doctor could often get a larger payment from the insurance company by charging a higher price, with no adverse consequence to either the doctor or the patient. In the same way, so the argument would go, presenting a needy student with a bigger tuition bill would simply lead to a bigger federal payment, benefiting the institution without harming the student.

There can be little doubt that according to any plausible model of institutional behavior, colleges would tend to act this way when they could. And the fact that federal aid dollars are keyed to student financial need—which rises with tuition—makes it appear that colleges should be able to capture more federal aid by raising prices. However, the impression dissolves on closer inspection. In the main federal grant program, the Pell program, the amount of aid awarded to a student is a function of the student's need, up to a limit imposed by the student's family's income. Thus the largest grant any student can receive for 1997–98, no matter how needy, is $2,700, and maximum grant size declines with family income. At current Pell funding levels, these income-graded award maxima are a very severe constraint, with the result that virtually no students in private higher education and relatively few in public higher education have their full need met by Pell. And only in the rare case where Pell meets full need below the maximum would an increase in a college's tuition allow that student to receive a larger Pell grant.

Similarly, the campus-based programs are in principle limited by need, but at current funding levels, most campuses are already receiving the maximum funding from these programs that regulations allow, and higher tuition would not lead to any funding increase.

The most plausible place to look for an impact of tuition increases on available federal funds is in the federal loan programs. Even here, however, many students already receive maximum federal loans, particularly in the private sector. Moreover, should a school raise its tuition to qualify students for more loans, its clientele would bear a significant share of the burden of the tuition increase, as loan subsidies relieve only part of the cost of a loan.[1] At present, more students are below the loan maximum in the public sector than in the private sector, and it is therefore more likely that federal aid increases would drive tuition higher in public rather than in private institutions.

Thus a closer look at institutional details undermines the theoretical assumption that federal aid increases drive tuition increases, especially in private higher education.

An empirical study we have conducted (reported in McPherson and Schapiro 1991b, ch. 4) reinforces this skeptical conclusion. We built a model that examined the interactions among a number of financial variables at individual colleges and universities. We did not limit our model to the relationship between tuition levels and federal aid, for two reasons. First, we judged that there were a number of other relationships of interest in the data. Federal financial aid may, for example, influence the amount of money schools devote to instruction; alternatively, federal aid may replace student aid funding from the schools' own resources or else, like a matching grant, induce them to spend more of their own resources on student aid. For that matter, federal spending to support research may well leak over into other areas, affecting the price and quality of undergraduate instruction. Second, to estimate accurately the relationship between any two variables in an interactive system, it is necessary to consider them in the context of the full set of interactions.

We used federally collected data on the finances of individual institutions for the years 1978–79 and 1985–86 in our statistical analysis.[2] We estimated relations between changes in the levels of funding from various sources and changes in universities' and colleges' financial behavior. The analysis focused on explaining three financial variables over which institutions have control: their spending per student on institution-based aid, their level of gross tuition and fees per student, and their level of instructional expenditures per student. The external financing variables fell into three categories: revenue from government, revenue derived from private gifts and endowment income, and revenue generated by the institutions' pricing and aid policies.

We found no evidence of the "Bennett hypothesis," that private institutions increased their tuitions when they received more federal student aid, nor was there a significant impact of changes in federal student aid on changes in instructional spending at private institutions. For public institutions, the effects of federal student aid differed in important ways from what we found at private institutions. We did not find any significant relationship between federal aid and instructional expenditures. We did, however, find that public four-year institutions tended to raise tuition by $50 for every $100 increase in federal student aid. As noted earlier, the institutional details make it more plausible for public than for private institutions to respond to increases in federal aid by raising tuition. Recall, however, that these results are based on data ending in the mid-1980s. Given the tuition increases that have occurred in public higher education since then, it is likely that fewer institutions could gain federal student aid revenue by increasing tuition, and we would not be surprised to discover that the effect of federal aid on public tuition has been substantially attenuated by now.

Our data permitted us to investigate not only the hypothesis that increases in federal student aid cause tuition increases but also the hypothesis that federal student aid increases cause reductions in institutional student aid commitments, as federal aid substitutes for need-based student aid. Although no significant relationship between institution-based aid and federal student aid emerged at public institutions, we found that private institutions tended to *increase* their spending on institution-based aid when federal student aid increased. Specifically, private colleges and universities increased institutional financial aid by $20 for every $100 increase in federal student aid.

This positive impact of federal aid on institution-based aid is somewhat surprising, given that one might expect that institutions would use federal aid to offset the cost of their own aid. That approach, however, assumes that the set of students recruited by the institution is not sensitive to these aid policies. A different possibility is that the availability of federal aid encourages students of lesser means to go to college and encourages colleges to admit them, with the result that schools wind up admitting a needier clientele, which in turn draws more heavily on the institution's own aid resources. Although further testing of the reliability of this finding is called for, it does suggest a very positive potential role for federal aid. If indeed private institutions tend to match federal contributions to needy students with their own dollars, this provides significant leverage for federal commitments—a point we will return to later.

It is important to be clear about what these findings do and do not indicate about the effects of incentives on college and university behavior. The findings do not show that higher education institutions are insensitive to incentives; a more plausible interpretation of the lack of response to private college tuition to federal aid levels is that there have not in fact been very large incentives present for colleges to change their pricing and aid behavior when federal aid policy changes have occurred.

Current Federal Policy Initiatives

We thus find that in the present environment, changes in spending on federal grants have not produced large effects on the financial behavior of colleges and states, simply because the incentives to change have not been strong. However, large, discontinuous changes in federal policy could alter this institutional environment considerably and thus might well generate significant incentives for colleges, universities, and state governments to change their behavior.

The most prominent policy proposals at the time of this writing are the tax proposals that have been advanced by the Clinton administration in its budget for fiscal 1998. Although these proposals, at least in detail, probably have a short half-life, they are worth examining closely because in fact there is every reason to believe that the incentive effects of such proposals are mightily affected by the details. The president has offered a two-part tax proposal: a nonrefundable 100% credit up to $1,500 per student for tuition expenses for students in their first two years of college and a tax deduction of up to $10,000 per taxpayer unit for postsecondary education and training expenses. Taxpayers can elect which tax preference they prefer to use. Both tax preferences recognize only tuition and not room and board as qualifying expenses. To receive the credit in the second year of college, a student must earn a B− average in the first year; no such requirement attaches to the deduction. Joint filers are eligible for the full credit or deduction if their incomes are below $80,000; the eligible maximum is reduced to 0 as income rises to $100,000. The deduction is "above the line"—taxpayers do not need to itemize to receive it. Importantly, the size of the tax credit available to a student is limited by the number of federal student aid dollars the student receives: each dollar of student aid grant reduces eligibility for the tax credit by a dollar. Thus even if a student had net educational expenses of $1,500 after accounting for all sources of aid, the student's family would not receive any tax credit if $1,500 of the aid received was from the federal government. The net effect of these provisions is to ensure that low-income students at low-cost institutions are unlikely to receive any benefit from the new tax provisions; the largest tax benefits will accrue to families in the $60,000 to $80,000 range whose children attend expensive private colleges (see Gladieux 1997).

We will discuss the desirability of this kind of targeting of federal resources, along with broader questions about using the tax system as a device for aiding students, in Chapter 14. Here our focus is on incentive effects.

First, would these new tax provisions tend to cause colleges to raise tuition prices? Effects of the tax credit provision are likely to be limited. Some states still have community college systems in which average tuition is below $1,500. To the extent that these schools have populations that qualify for the full $1,500 credit, they will certainly have incentives to raise tuition to that level. However, these schools also have important constituencies of part-time and low-income independent students who are unlikely to benefit from the credit, and those constituencies will continue to press for low tuition.

The situation would be considerably different if, as in a Senate Democrat version of the president's bill, students are allowed to receive both a Pell grant and a tax credit. Then students could be eligible for as much as $4,200 in aid from Pell and the tax credit combined, and that total exceeds tuition costs at a large number of public institutions.

The proposed tax deduction is likely to have larger incentive effects than the tax credit. Most public institutions (though very few private ones) have tuition below $10,000. Making tuition tax-deductible would imply that for eligible families, the federal government will pay between 15% and 28% of any tuition increase, depending on the family's tax bracket. This would be a significant easing of the burden of higher tuition for families in income ranges of roughly $40,000 to $100,000—a quite important constituency for public universities. The political processes that underlie the setting of tuition are certainly complicated ones, but we suspect that these incentives will be significant.[3]

What about the likely impact of these tax preferences on institutions' and state governments' provision of student aid? We suspect that the incentive effects are likely to be quite strong. The standard methodology for determining family ability to pay for college should take the added resources provided by these tax breaks into account in determining financial need. There are actually two different ways in which colleges and state student aid agencies might interpret these added resources. In one interpretation, the increase in family after-tax income could simply be seen as added after-tax earning power, similar to any other tax cut a family might receive. In that case, the reduction in family need would be a fraction of the increase in after-tax income, that fraction being determined by the marginal taxing rate within the student aid system. A family earning $60,000 to $80,000 per year that was eligible for state or institutional aid would be expected to contribute about 44% of the tax break in the form of increased family ability to pay. In a second interpretation, the college tax break might be viewed as an added resource dedicated to college, much like an outside scholarship. In that case, standard methodology would say that all of the added after-tax income should be devoted to educational expenses, and the family's aid from the state or the institution would be reduced dollar for dollar against proceeds of the tax credit or deduction.

Our conclusion that schools would substitute tax break dollars for their own student aid dollars is different from the empirical finding we reported earlier—that schools increased their own aid spending when Pell spending increased. However, in that case we suggested that this result was explained by the fact that schools were induced by the added Pell availability to recruit more needy students, who then got institution-based aid as well as Pells. Unfortunately, the tax provisions proposed by the Clinton administration are not targeted at the high-need students whose college-going behavior is most likely to be influenced by reductions in cost of attendance. We therefore conclude that schools and states are likely to absorb much of the benefit of the tax cuts themselves.

Whether such a transfer from the federal government to state governments and individual private institutions is desirable is a separate question. Although some private colleges and universities would get significant revenues from readjusting their student aid calculations, the bulk of the transfer is likely to be toward public colleges and universities and state governments. This is mainly because that is where most of the students are but also because these institutions will have incentives to raise prices as well as to recalculate aid.

Thus from one point of view, the Clinton proposals could be seen to a significant extent as an intergovernmental transfer, a federal effort to relieve overstressed state budgets. Indeed, it is interesting that the proposed federal revenue loss through these tax cuts of around $7 billion per year is of the same order of magnitude as the reduction in real support of public higher education by state governments during the 1990s. The president's proposed program would partly relieve families of the added financing burden generated by this reduction in state support and would partly create an environment that encourages further withdrawal of state support.

It is unlikely that advocates of this course intend this result. In principle, a good case can be made for shifting the major burden of government financing of higher education from the state to the federal level (a case we have in fact made in McPherson and Schapiro 1991b). But at a time when budgetary resources are scarce at all levels of government, it seems desirable to design programs that encourage state and federal governments to be partners in financing higher education rather than programs that encourage one level of government to replace the efforts of another.

An obvious alternative to these tax proposals would be to spend equivalent amounts of revenue on expanding the Pell grant program, perhaps in modified form. Senator Paul Wellstone has proposed raising the Pell grant maximum to $5,000. A more modest program that would put the 1998–99 Pell grant maximum at roughly its 1979–80 level would call for a $4,000 maximum Pell. What would be the incentive effects of such a policy change?

Clearly, such increases would provide low-cost public colleges with incentives to raise tuition. These incentives are, however, attenuated by two important factors. First, unlike the tax break proposals, which recognize only tuition as an educational cost, Pell grant budgets reflect living expenses as well as tuition. Thus even with a $4,000 or $5,000 maximum, relatively few schools could make their students eligible for more aid by raising tuition. Moreover, again unlike the tax proposals, Pell grants are designed to decline with increases in family income. Thus even with a larger maximum, relatively fewer students will be able to qualify for larger awards through tuition increases because the awards available to most students are limited by income to well below the maximum.

Incentives for schools to reduce their own student aid awards as Pell awards grow are clearly present, much as with the tax proposals. However, increased Pell awards are much more likely to induce more relatively low-income, high-need students to attend college than would happen with the tax cuts. The presence of more such students would likely induce schools and states to spend more of their own resources on student aid, thus at least partially—and conceivably more than fully—offsetting the tendency to substitute higher federal aid for state and institution-based resources.

It is interesting to inquire whether the federal government might be more proactive in forging a partnership with states and institutions. If the federal government is indeed ready to expand its contributions to higher education financing, are there ways to do that while encouraging the other players in the system to maintain or even increase their own efforts?

Attempts by the federal government to mandate the behavior of state governments and individual actors have, for generally good reasons, met an increasingly chilly reception. Certainly the ability of the federal government to manage the pricing and aid decisions of states and individual colleges directly is minimal at best. Price controls or the like as the cost of greater federal involvement in higher education would be an unworthy bargain and an imprudent line of march for the government.

There may, however, be ways for the federal government to use its considerable financial leverage to produce incentives that will encourage schools and states to direct their policies toward desirable goals.[4]

This is not the place to put forward a fully developed policy proposal for such an intervention. Any such design would need to attend to many complications reflecting variations in the circumstances of individual colleges and states. The following policy sketch may, however, usefully illustrate the possibilities.

Suppose that rather than increasing the Pell grant, as some have advocated, the federal government instead introduced a new grant program "piggybacked" on top of Pell. These new grants would be means-tested, like Pell, but would also include a new institution eligibility requirement. For a school's students to be eligible for the new "access" grants, the school would have to demonstrate that it met at least 90% of the financial need of all full-time, dependent undergraduate students from families with incomes below $40,000 per year. Need would be calculated according to federal formulas and would be met by a combination of grants, loans, and work, with the amounts met by loan and work bounded by upper limits.

Such a grant program would have some desirable properties. For private institutions, it would ensure that significant institutional aid resources were being allocated to the neediest among its students. Setting the requirement at 90% of all full need (or some other reasonable figure) would guard against making the requirement overly precise and would also help discourage the possibility that schools would avoid admitting high-need students in order to make the requirement easier to meet.

For public institutions, this program would require one of two things. One option would be for a state to keep its tuition at public institutions low enough for all students to make it feasible for these relatively low-income students to have their needs met through available resources. Alternatively, a state that chose to raise tuition would need to "recycle" enough of the added tuition dollars to keep college affordable for its low-income families.

Many variations on this basic idea are of course feasible and worthy of discussion. This proposal, for example, is silent on independent and part-time students, simply because full-time dependent students are the easiest group to define and the one for which conventional measures of ability to pay are most adequate. We would argue that proposals on these lines, which recognize explicitly the need for partnership among states, individual schools, and the federal government, should be a prominent part of future discussions of federal higher education policy.

Conclusion

It is a mistake to view higher education institutions simply as passive instruments that transmit government policies. Especially in this time of heightened strategic consciousness and pressure on resources, colleges and universities are actively managing their aid and pricing policies. Analyses of policy options that neglect institutional reactions are likely to be badly off base. At the same time, taking explicit account of the reactions of institutions to policy may be a positive tool in government programs. Policies designed to elicit socially desirable responses from institutions can provide needed leverage for the achievement of desired results. This point is all the more important given the limitations on federal funding and the relatively modest role it plays in the overall higher education financing system.

9

Student Aid as a Competitive Weapon

As WE ARGUED briefly in Chapter 2, colleges' growing reliance on student aid policies as a strategic instrument for managing enrollment and revenues is more a matter of circumstances and incentives than it is of any rejection of the "moral" principles that lie behind need-based aid. The handful of schools that practice a "need-blind, full-need" approach to financial aid are distinguished mainly by the exceptional resources, both of endowment and of affluent high-quality applicants, that allow them to sustain the practice. Moreover, as we will argue here, adherence to these policies serves their interests very well, and it would serve their interests even better if other schools were made to conform to those policies. When representatives of this relatively privileged set of institutions advocates "need-blind, full-need" policies for all of higher education, their position is both impractical and, in some measure, even if unconsciously, self-serving.

The simple morality of the "need-blind, full-need" approach is both too simple and too limited to provide a general guide to colleges and universities in shaping their aid policies. Does this then mean that all moral bets are off, that "anything goes" in the student aid marketplace, with the only ethic being *caveat emptor?* This, we think, is too simple and not ethically demanding enough. Our aim in this chapter is to try to contribute to more realistic and constructive thinking about the proprieties of student aid policies. To do that, however, we must lay some groundwork by providing a more concrete and specific sense of how the strategic aspects of student aid policy are managed in practice.[1]

To that end, we have constructed a stylized but still instructive example. Table 9.1 provides admissions and aid statistics for the class of 2000 at the mythical Conjectural University, a moderately selective private institution that practices need-blind admissions and full-need funding of enrolled students. The table cross-classifies the applicant pool according to ability to pay and academic promise (measured here for convenience simply by combined SAT scores). Within each academic ability and financial need group, the table reports the number of applicants, the number accepted, and the number enrolling. The table gives a rich picture of how the combined

TABLE 9.1
Admissions Profile, Conjectural University

Combined SAT Score	No Need			Low Need (Grant: 0–$5,000)			Medium Need (Grant: $5,000–$12,500)			High Need (Grant: $12,500–$25,000)			Total		
	Apply	Accept	Enroll	Apply	Accept	Enroll	Apply	Accept	Enroll	Apply	Accept	Enroll	Apply	Accept	Enroll
1300+	75	75	20	75	75	25	75	75	30	60	60	30	285	285	105
1100–1300	125	110	40	125	110	45	125	110	50	125	110	60	500	440	195
900–1100	300	250	75	300	250	80	300	250	90	300	250	100	1,200	1,000	345
700–900	300	200	80	300	200	80	300	200	80	300	200	90	1,200	800	330
Below 700	400	10	9	400	10	9	400	10	9	400	10	9	1,600	40	36
Total	1,200	645	224	1,200	645	239	1,200	645	259	1,185	630	289	4,785	2,565	1,011
Average SAT	866	1018	988	866	1018	1003	866	1018	1015	858	1008	1013	864	1016	1006

policies of the admissions and aid offices wind up producing the freshman class.

As the summary data at the bottom of the table show, Conjectural enrolls a freshman class of 1,011 students by admitting 2,565 out of an applicant pool of 4,785. The selectivity of the place is evidenced in the fact that the average SAT score of the freshman class (1006) is substantially above that of the applicant pool (864). Although the data are pure fiction, they reflect some realistic features of actual schools. Thus, for example, higher-ability students are generally more likely to be admitted and less likely to enroll than lower-ability students. High-need students are more likely to enroll if admitted and, at a need-blind place, are no less likely to be admitted, given equal ability levels.

The real use of a table like this lies in examining the consequences of potential changes in admissions and aid policies. Suppose that Conjectural had formulated a goal of raising the number of high-ability students in the class (perhaps because the current situation reflected a fall from a more glorious past) and that a board member stood ready to put up enough cash to support a big investment in this effort. An obvious thing to try would be raising the "yield" of high-ability, low- or no-need students by offering merit scholarships. Suppose that Conjectural were to offer $10,000 merit scholarships to no-need students in the applicant pool from the 1300+ SAT group. This might yield, say, ten new students. Notice that the cost of the program in the first year would be not only the $100,000 going to the newly attracted students but an additional $200,000 to the students who would have enrolled anyway (since there is no way to figure out in advance which ones they are). If this program were sustained for each new class through its four years at Conjectural, its cost once fully implemented would be $1.2 million per year.

But there is an obvious way to offset some of that cost. With ten high-ability students added to the class, the college could reduce its admission of other students by ten, and the obvious place to look would be in the low-ability, high-need group. If the college simply rejected the ten students it now accepts from that group, it would avoid financial aid expenditures on them of about $17,500 per student for nine students, or $157,500. Over four classes, this would amount to annual savings of $630,000, offsetting just about half the cost of the merit aid program. The net effect on average SATs of replacing these high-need, low-ability students with high-ability, no-need students would be a gain of about 8 points.

Whether this would be a prudent, clever, or fair thing to do is a matter we will address shortly, but first consider another possible policy change. Suppose that rather than looking for higher-quality students, the institution was instead in a bind that compelled it to look for savings in its financial aid operation. Again, the obvious strategy would be to deny admission to high-need, low-ability students and replace them with students of lower need. For concreteness, imagine a dramatic change. Suppose that Conjectural simply stopped admitting high-need applicants with SATs below 900—a more dramatic step than a real college would likely take. This would cut enrollment by ninety-nine. Suppose, for simplicity, that the college replaced those ninety-nine by admitting more no-need students. In particular, suppose they admitted all no-need students with SATs above 900, admitted another fifty from the 700–900 range, and admitted enough with SATs below 700 to make up the remainder of the enrollment shortfall produced by denying admission to the high-need, low-ability students. Assuming constant yield rates for these applicant groups, the results of this policy shift are shown in Table 9.2. Notice that the average SAT scores of enrolled no-need students fall sharply, from 988 to 910, but that this drop is partly offset by a rise from 1013 to 1134 in the average SATs of high-need students. On balance, the effect on average SATs for the entering class is a drop of 5 points—achieved, however, by more than doubling the number of students in the class with very low SATs. The financial savings are spectacular—about $1.75 million in the first year, or $7 million per year once the effects work through the four years.

Such a policy is too draconian to be realistic, but notice that a milder version of the policy might be plausible. Suppose that the college rejected the ten lowest-ranking students among its high-need applicants and replaced them with the highest-ranking among the no-need students it would otherwise reject. The effect on the quality of the class might be minimal, and the first-year financial savings would be $175,000.

Policies of this kind—making admission need-aware or introducing merit aid—obviously have great appeal to hard-pressed colleges. An analysis like that in Tables 9.1 and 9.2 makes the options and the trade-offs they imply relatively clear. Real-world admission and aid strategies differ from this stylized example mainly in increasing the dimensionality of the problem, adding to the number of ways in which the prospects presented to different students are manipulated.

Perhaps the most important of these, in terms of the frequency with which it is employed in American higher education, is known as "differential packaging." Even now, relatively few of the more selective institutions in American higher education are eager to own up to the practice of offering "no-need" aid. However, differential treatment of

TABLE 9.2
Revised Admissions Policy, Conjectural University

Combined SAT Score	No Need			Low Need (Grant: 0–$5,000)			Medium Need (Grant: $5,000–$12,500)			High Need (Grant: $12,500–$25,000)			Total		
	Apply	Accept	Enroll	Apply	Accept	Enroll	Apply	Accept	Enroll	Apply	Accept	Enroll	Apply	Accept	Enroll
1300+	75	75	20	75	75	25	75	75	30	60	60	30	285	285	105
1100–1300	125	125	45	125	110	45	125	110	50	125	110	60	500	455	200
900–1100	300	300	90	300	250	80	300	250	90	300	250	100	1,200	1,050	360
700–900	300	250	100	300	200	80	300	200	80	300	0	0	1,200	650	260
Below 700	400	75	68	400	10	9	400	10	9	400	0	0	1,600	95	86
Total	1,200	825	323	1,200	645	239	1,200	645	259	1,185	420	190	4,785	2,535	1,011
Average SAT	866	974	910	866	1018	1003	866	1018	1015	858	1117	1134	864	1020	1001

students within the aid-eligible population is very common. As we noted in Chapter 2, this practice takes the form of offering a sweeter aid package—more grant, less loan and work—to students who are found for one reason or another to be more promising. It is odd that even among schools where the award of pure merit or no-need aid would be anathema, differential packaging is accepted as a natural fact of life.

Just one step beyond differential packaging is a practice known in the business as "gapping." With differential packaging, every needy admitted student is offered an aid package that theoretically meets full need. Of course, that may be theoretical indeed if the package includes a requirement for the student and parents to borrow, say, $8,000 a year for four years. Under a gapping strategy, the claim that need is being met is dropped, and students will be offered aid packages that meet only a specified percentage of need. The student is then invited to try to come up with the difference between what his or her family was judged able to pay and what they will actually have to pay to attend. Some students will take up this invitation, perhaps by stretching the family budget or perhaps by the good luck of having a friendly aunt or grandfather who will help pay the bills. Obviously, schools that practice gapping generally meet a larger percentage of the need of more attractive students.

A first cousin of gapping is "admit-deny." Students are admitted regardless of financial need, but marginal students are then denied financial aid. Doing this allows a school to proclaim that it is "need-blind" in admissions. The admissions office under this system can indeed ignore student ability to pay, but that criterion then returns with a vengeance as the financial aid office decides which students will have the wherewithal actually to attend. Schools following admit-deny strategies would no doubt assert that at least they are giving these students an opportunity to come up with a generous grandparent or two. But the reality is that under both admit-deny and gapping, one of the worst aspects of preferential aid packaging comes to the forefront: the weakest students get saddled with loans and part-time work that make their already tenuous graduation prospects even lower.

An alternative, when aid money is too scarce to meet full need for all qualified applicants, is to adopt a policy of "need-aware second review." For students on a second review list (either a formal waiting list or any delayed-admission list), one of the characteristics considered in getting admitted is parents' ability to pay. Schools following this approach plainly are not fully "need-blind," but they do often claim to be by stressing that students who meet the normal criteria for admissibility are admitted on a "need-blind, fully met need" basis.

But why would schools follow this approach rather than admit-deny or gapping? Don't they have an interest in capturing some of those students who would be denied financial aid but would nevertheless come up with the money and matriculate? The usual response is that the school doesn't want to encourage these students to undertake undue financial burdens. There may be something to this appeal to paternalism, but it is not the full story. It seems more plausible that these schools recognize that admitting needy students without financial aid means that a few will come but most will not. What that means is that the school will be forced to admit a greater percentage of its applicants to make up for the decline in yield. But the ratio of applicants to admits is one of the main ways that rating services and national newsmagazines keep score in determining which are the "best" schools. One result is that schools try hard not to admit students who probably won't come, an effort that is said sometimes to extend to calling students on the waiting list to find out if they will come before deciding whether to admit them. But plainly admitting needy students with no aid is a surefire way to reduce the school's yield of matriculants from among accepted applicants and thereby to risk harming the school's standing. Moreover, admitting needy students while denying them aid can be as much a cruel joke as a gesture toward fairness. Schools may well produce more ill will among applicants by an admit-deny strategy than by a need-aware admissions strategy.

Schools differentiate themselves not only by adopting various combinations of the strategies described here but also by varying the ways in which they implement those strategies. The procedures used to calculate need are an important source of variation. Schools that receive financial aid from the federal government are constrained to some degree by law in the methods they can use for computing financial need for all of their students (not only those who receive federal aid). But these roles are only broadly constraining and leave room for "professional judgment." Thus some colleges and universities count the equity a family has in their home as an asset available to be "taxed" for student aid purposes, while others ignore or limit home equity in determining ability to pay. Similarly, some institutions treat the cost of sending younger children in the family to private schools as a legitimate expense in computing family ability to pay, while others do not. Wide variation in the treatment of divorced parents produces further divergences. These differing practices can easily produce differences of several thousands of dollars between schools in their calculations of families' ability to pay. Such discretion can also creep into the treatment of different students within the same school as well as across schools. In principle, the standards of professional judgment within an institution are supposed to be insensitive to differences in the desirability of students, but the fact is that it would be very difficult to detect a school that calculated need more generously for students that it strongly wanted to recruit.

It is hard to generalize about the effectiveness of these various financial aid strategies in promoting individual institutions' goals. A great deal will obviously depend on the circumstances of the individual institution. However, one broad generalization will stand up: the consequences for any one school of following these kinds of aid strategies will differ greatly, depending on how their fellow institutions respond. This is most obviously true of merit aid and differential aid packaging strategies. Consider an individual school with four or five close competitors with overlapping admissions pools. If this institution offers selective price cuts in the form of merit aid or "sweetened" aid packages to its most promising students while its competitors do not, the impact on the institution's yield of these desirable students is likely to be quite strong. But if the school's price cuts have this effect, it is likely that they will provoke a response from the competing institutions. In terms of the example discussed earlier, if Conjectural University recruits ten top students through merit aid, there is a good chance that it is recruiting them away from a few close competitors. If the College of the Imagination, just down the street from Conjectural, notices the loss and figures out the reason, it is very likely to respond with an equally or more aggressive merit aid program than Conjectural's. It's easy to picture a chain reaction that ends up with all the schools in the area enrolling basically the same students they would enroll without their merit aid programs but forgoing a lot of tuition revenue from them (not unlike the airline industry in a price war).

A different but equally potent dynamic can result from a single school's adopting a need-aware admissions strategy or a strategy of gapping or admit-deny. Competitor schools who don't follow suit will encounter an abrupt increase in the fraction of relatively high-need, low-quality admitted students who choose to enroll, for suddenly the competitors' admissions and aid offers will have become relatively more attractive. Thus the decision by any one school to worsen the offers it makes to high-need students will increase the pressure on competing schools to do the same. There is, however, an important difference between this case and the case of merit aid or differential packaging. For here, while there is clearly harm to the interests of the students whose aid offers are being worsened or withdrawn, there is no harm to the collective financial interests of the schools involved, as there is in the case of a merit aid price war.

All this calculation and manipulation is disturbing and leads natu-
rally for a wish to achieve (some would say return to) admissions and
aid practices of greater simplicity and purity. These demands come
particularly easily to the lips of admissions and aid officers at the
most selective institutions and to those of high school guidance counselors who bear the burden of advising students on college choices. Yet
in both groups, the advice must be taken with at least a grain of salt.

Leading institutions such as members of the Ivy League were
among the original architects of the need-based aid system. Under
ideal conditions, a fully functioning need-based aid system would re-
move ability to pay as a factor in students' college choices. The family
of a particular student would be asked to pay what it could, as determined by an objective analysis of the family's ability to pay. If
that analysis was uniform across institutions, the family's obligation
would be the same regardless of what institution the student attended. There is undoubtedly much that is attractive about this image
of how the student financing system should work. However, several
factors undermine the force of the claims in its favor, especially when
that system is advocated by the most affluent and selective places.

First, even this system still leaves room for differential packaging of
aid, a very important source of differences across institutions in what
it costs particular students to attend.

Second, an argument from leading institutions that all institutions
should follow their policies neglects the very real difference in circumstances of different institutions. An institution with an endowment per student of $50,000 and an entering class in which 75% of the
students pay full price is taking on a much lighter burden in commit-
ting to "need-blind, full-need" than a school with an endowment of
$3,000 per student and 75% of the class on aid.

Finally, it is possible to bring a different perspective to the argument that the "need-blind, full-need" approach to student aid "levels
the playing field" by eliminating relative cost as a factor in students'
choice of college. This alternative perspective takes off from the fact
that the most highly selective schools offer quite substantial subsidies
to all their students (see Winston 1996). Endowment and gift resources for such institutions may contribute as much as $20,000 per
student or more to covering the cost of education. Because these affluent schools admit only students with very strong qualifications, it is
possible to argue that every student at such a school is receiving a
substantial merit scholarship. Less well endowed schools might argue
that in offering better aid packages or merit scholarships to their
strongest applicants, they are simply trying to match the subsidies
offered by their wealthier colleagues.

Yet this kind of analysis also brings to the fore questions about the long-run financial wisdom as well as the ethical propriety of such policies. The right answers for particular institutions depend very much on local circumstances and options, but we believe that the following general points should be kept in mind when contemplating such policies.

First, colleges should not think themselves obliged to meet goals that are simply beyond their financial capacity. The handful of schools that practice both need-blind admissions and full-need funding of aid for enrolled students are in a highly favorable position to honor such claims. They are very well endowed places with the added benefit of having large numbers of affluent full-pay students. There is no more fundamental constraint on ethical principles than *"ought* implies *can"*—no one can be morally obliged to do what is beyond one's powers. It is our sense that colleges and universities should view the effort to extend opportunities for access to their educational offerings as an important goal, but not one that must override all other goals, such as offering a high-quality education to those who do attend.

In this context, it is important to recognize that simply being "need-blind" in admissions, absent the resources required to meet the need of all who enroll, is an empty goal. Once a college finds that it must ration student aid funds, the question of how this is best done becomes a matter of strategy and judgment. A school might, for example, admit without regard to need but then deny financial aid to the lower-ranked and needier among the admitted students. Or it might offer the less attractive among the needy admits financial aid packages that fall short of meeting need (a gapping strategy). Or it might make the admission decision itself need-aware. There is no obvious principle that makes one of these strategies more moral than another.

Indeed, there are times when being self-consciously need-aware may be more effective for a school that is trying to promote greater economic diversity among its student body than a need-blind strategy would be. This is obviously the case if a school wants to use information about financial need to admit a more economically needy class than need-blindness would yield. But it is also quite plausible to imagine that a school in particular circumstances could find that being purely need-blind is not producing the income profile it desires and that it could produce a better result by "tilting" in favor of middle-income students or in favor of high-need students.

Although the moral choices colleges face are complex, there is, in our view, one moral principle that should be widely respected in schools' admissions policies. This is the principle of honesty. Schools should inform applicants and high school guidance counselors of how they make their decisions. There is a good deal of pressure on schools to maintain a claim to being need-blind when the reality of their policies is more complicated. Many schools, for example, are need-blind for freshman admits but not for transfers, and others, as we have noted, are need-blind for the first round of admits but need-aware on the waiting list. Schools should be explicit about such policies.

Conclusion

In this chapter, we applied some basic economic approaches in the analysis of what has become known as enrollment management. Colleges and universities have become much more sophisticated in their use of tuition discounting and creative financial aid packaging in order to serve their many objectives—whether the principal goal is maximization of net tuition revenue, the enhancement of widely reported selectivity indicators (raising average SATs, lowering the admit rate, and so on), or an increase in the diversity of the student body.

Of course, colleges typically have multiple objectives. Even Conjectural University, should it follow one of the net tuition strategies described here—rejecting the ten lowest-ranking students among its high-need applicants and replacing them with the highest-ranking students among the no-need students it would otherwise reject—would experience a decrease in the economic diversity of the entering class along with some decline in average SAT. Is that an acceptable trade-off? Careful economic analysis can identify the options open to a particular school, but it is up to educational leaders and their constituencies (boards of trustees, students, alumni, faculty, and sometimes the general public) to determine the right path to follow.

As we argued, underlying our discussion of the most responsible way to apply economic principles to higher education is the desirability of being clear and honest about what you are doing. Increasing numbers of colleges and universities are not meeting that standard. Stecklow (1996) describes how the application of sophisticated enrollment management analysis leads institutions to offer inferior financial aid packages to unsuspecting prospective students that seem particularly interested in attending the institution (coming for a campus tour and the like), and Shea (1996) discusses how institutions manage to offer desirable students all sorts of extra financial incentives while continuing to celebrate their "need-blind" admissions policies. Is there anything wrong with either of these institutional policies? It depends on the particular context. But the alleged duplicity involved is troubling.

There is also the problem of the many schools who are adopting a policy of "need-aware second review"—using need-blind admissions for applicants who are clearly admissible but considering financial need for more marginal applicants. There is a moral dilemma these schools must face: Do they tell their wait-listed students (or, for increasing numbers of schools, their transfer applicants) that the failure to withdraw their financial aid applications means that their chances of admission are between slim and none? We might insist once again that honesty is the best policy. But schools are eager to avoid the negative publicity that comes with acknowledging that in some real sense students are able to "buy their way into the school." Hence it is no surprise that high school counselors report that it is very difficult to get a straight answer to a straight question: "Does my needy, wait-listed student actually have a chance to get in?"

We have argued here that the best defense of need-aware admissions policies is that there is nothing ethical about keeping a policy that drives the school to financial insolvency, forcing it to sacrifice instruction, basic student services, and other essentials. When financial distress or competitive pressures are real, this is a perfectly legitimate argument—although it is not an argument that justifies dishonesty about the practices being followed. The argument is less compelling when it is used by schools with large endowments and strong market positions: if you give up your moral commitments too easily, you provoke doubt about just how deep they were in the first place.

The question of honesty in what schools are actually doing was brought home to us recently when we had the opportunity to review financial aid award letters from dozens of schools over a number of years. It is striking how slippery they have become. Even as alleged experts on financial aid, we were often hard pressed to figure out what was being offered. Was full need being met? Just how large a loan was the student and family being asked to take on? When recruitment pressures make financial aid letters look like they are written by the same people who write the marketing brochure, we are all in trouble.

The coming years will not bring any painless solutions to the moral dilemmas posed by increasing pressure on financial aid budgets. Competitive pressures push schools toward a least-common-denominator result: if the college down the block writes a misleading aid award letter, then it's OK for you to do so too; if your best students are being picked off with generous merit awards from other institutions, you should feel free to join the game. Nobody should expect college administrators to be saints who will turn the other cheek when they are smitten by competition. Yet if all our commitments to marketing and financial success overwhelm colleges' adherence to principle in the financial aid arena, the American people will have been given one more reason to lose their respect for higher education.

Part Four

THE SPECIAL CASE OF MERIT AID

THIS PART builds on our ongoing analysis of merit aid (McPherson and Schapiro 1994). Scattered evidence suggests that the share of all institution-based student aid funds going to merit aid has been rising sharply over the past decade. Anecdotal evidence suggests that merit competition is particularly intense among relatively prestigious universities of the "second tier" and among liberal arts colleges in the Midwest that are facing enrollment declines and increasingly severe public-sector price competition. Some observers expect the end of "overlap agreements" to cause merit scholarship competition to spread more widely among elite institutions as well. These trends seem very important to understand.

Chapter 10 begins with a review of the history of merit aid. It goes on to examine the social implications of merit aid expenditures, addressing the broad question, What are the consequences of merit aid practices for the quality and distribution of educational opportunity in the United States? Data sets that have not previously been employed in this context are used to determine what kinds of institutions invest in merit aid (Chapter 11) and what kinds of students are likely to receive merit aid (Chapter 12). Whenever possible, changes over time in the distribution of merit aid are considered. The part concludes in Chapter 13 with a summary of the positive and negative aspects of merit aid.

10 _____

Merit Aid

ITS PLACE IN HISTORY AND ITS ROLE IN SOCIETY

History of Merit Aid

Reviewing the historical evolution of student aid in American higher education provides a useful background for the analysis of merit aid that follows. In fact, it also gives some perspective on our discussion of need-based aid in Part Three and on our view of the future in Part Five.

A highly informative summary of student aid history is contained in a paper by Philip G. Wick, the director of financial aid at Williams College (Wick 1993).[1]

Wick points out that student aid in the United States has existed far longer than most people assume. Brademas (1983) dates the establishment of the first institutional scholarship fund in America to a 1643 gift of £100 to Harvard College to support the education of a needy student. The 1983 president's report from Princeton University (written by President William Bowen) points out that the first known scholarship there was given to a member of the Class of 1759, a recipient who in turn established his own scholarship fund for needy students. Williams College's fund for "indigent young men of merit" is an example of the "charity funds" that were in place by the early 1800s, and Wick concludes that "since the beginning of the academy, scholarships have been used to attract students known or perceived to be needy and deserving" (p. 2).

A new era for student aid was launched after the Civil War, with state legislatures enhancing scholarship opportunities at state universities and land-grant colleges and benefactors endowing scholarships at private colleges. Charity funds were replaced by scholarship funds, but it is important to note that the key criterion remained neediness, not academic potential. Wick provides insight into how colleges and universities historically drew the line between need-based and merit aid by quoting from a 1897 document he discovered in the Williams College Archives, an addendum to the "Comparative Table of Expenses and Scholarship Aid in New England Colleges."

At Amherst College, "scholarship aid is awarded by a committee of the faculty. No special mark is set as essential for a student to attain in order to obtain beneficiary aid. The student must make formal application for aid—which must be signed by three persons, one of them his parent or guardian."

At Bowdoin College, "applications for scholarships must be made upon blank form, stating particularly the circumstances of the student. They must be made out anew each year. Of the 113 applications for scholarship aid in 1896, 31 were rejected."

At Brown, "the income of scholarships is given under the direction of a committee . . . to meritorious students who may need pecuniary assistance. In deserving cases tuition is sometimes remitted on application to the President."

At Dartmouth, "scholarships and beneficiary aid are awarded by a committee of the faculty. . . . Scholarships of $50 each are given as 'beneficiary aid' to students in need . . . with a rank of at least fifty per cent. The renewal of the application must be made every year and must be accompanied by a complete statement of income and expenditures during the year preceding. All [special academic] scholarships are open to those who need pecuniary aid."

At the University of Vermont, "applicants for scholarships must maintain a fair standing in scholarship, must furnish evidence of need and of desert, [and] must not indulge in tobacco or other expensive habits."

At Wesleyan, "a limited number of scholarships exempting the holders from the charge of tuition have been established by the Trustees . . . for the use of deserving students who need pecuniary assistance."

Finally, at Williams College, "students must make formal application for aid, must be needy, of good character, must avoid expensive habits and college discipline, [and] must attain a rank of at least sixty-five per cent."

In reviewing this evidence, Wick concludes that at the more selective and costly colleges, while financial aid was usually contingent on academic performance (during the twentieth century, students who fell below some minimum standard often had some or all of their grant aid replaced with loans or work opportunities), neediness was a necessary condition for scholarship consideration. A Williams College document from 1936–37 ("Report of the Secretary of the Committee on Student Aid") makes this point very clear: "Much thought and time is spent by the Student Aid Committee on studying the individual applications for scholarship and the financial situation of the applicant's family. Williams College has much to offer the boy of limited means and the administration of this Department as it pertains to scholarship grants, loans, and employment, carries with it much responsibility. The funds are not available to take care of all deserving applicants and from necessity the Committee must take awards where the need is greatest, of course taking into account the scholastic ability, character, and general promise of the candidate."[2]

A critical event in the history of financial aid in the United States was the creation in 1954 of the College Scholarship Service (CSS), as an extension of the College Board, by a group of ninety-five mostly northeastern private colleges and universities. The incentive behind this move appears to have been the avoidance of a bidding war for students. Although most of the members of this group had a long history of giving need-based aid, the goal of CSS was to apply a uniform methodology in the determination of financial need. At the same time, it ushered in an era in which admittance to college was based on merit but scholarship aid was almost exclusively awarded on the basis of need. Although, as mentioned, the experiences of certain elite colleges were heavily influenced by student need, Wick concludes that merit "often determined for many institutions which students, needy or not, were assisted" (p. 7). Thus it was of great significance, he argues, that the College Board endorsed the principle of need-based aid, and he attributes the dramatic increase in College Board membership after 1960 to the attraction of this stance to a growing body of colleges and universities.

Despite the influence of CSS, the awarding of scholarship aid based solely on the basis of merit continued to be a part of the American scene. Wick reviews a number of studies, including one by the director of financial aid at Stanford, R. Huff (1975), who reported that 54% of respondent institutions indicated that they were awarding some scholarships without any reference to financial need. Despite a reaffirmation of the principle of need-based aid by the College Scholarship Assembly of the College Board at its annual meeting in October 1976, Wick reviews evidence from subsequent surveys that the awarding of no-need academic scholarships and grants increased sharply.

With this background in mind, we turn next to a discussion of the social consequences of merit aid and then to our own analysis of recent changes over time in the prevalence of need-based versus merit aid.

Merit Aid and Society

The social consequences of merit aid are complex.[3] We find it helpful in sorting out the dimensions of the problem to contrast two aspects of the competitive forces that push schools toward merit aid. One of these is the attempt by schools of lesser reputation or quality to "buy" students from more prestigious schools through offers of merit aid. This kind of competitive effort redistributes students among institutions, with the effect of increasing the representation of lower-ranking students at less prestigious institutions and, more ambiguously, of reducing the representation of high-ranking students at more prestigious institutions.[4]

The other aspect is competition among schools of roughly equal quality or reputation for the most meritorious students in the schools' combined applicant pool. The individual school's aim here is to improve its relative position among a more or less well-defined group of peer institutions. Merit aid competition will move students within this group of schools but will not affect the overall distribution of high-ranking students by institutional quality. The main effect of merit aid here is to lower the net price paid by meritorious students for an education of given quality. Merit aid results in a redistribution of dollars between schools and students, rather than a systematic redistribution of students among schools.

Plainly, these two aspects of merit aid competition are entangled in reality. Analytically, however, they are worth distinguishing because they raise quite different social issues. If we focus on the second aspect of competition—that between peer institutions of similar quality—from the schools' point of view, merit aid wars can be seen as an instance of the "prisoners' dilemma." Each individual school tries to gain an advantage relative to its rivals by bidding down the price charged to high-quality students. But the net effect of this competitive effort is simply that all schools in the group match one another's offers and wind up with essentially the same group of students they would have had anyway but less net tuition revenue. If the schools could arrive at an enforceable agreement to abstain from merit aid, the allocation of students among schools would be unaffected, and the schools would have higher net revenues and hence be better off. This is the economic logic behind efforts by groups of schools like the Ivy League to arrive at agreements not to compete for students through merit aid awards.

Such agreements are plainly desirable for the schools involved, but are they socially desirable? The main social effect of merit competition among a group of peer institutions of similar quality is a redistribution of resources between the schools and students (or their families). On one hand, we need to ask whether increasing the incomes of families of high-ranking students is a desirable thing. On the other hand, we need to consider what activities the colleges will cut back on as a result of smaller net tuition revenues if they compete on merit aid.

Both of these are difficult judgments, but there is a good case to be made that the distribution of resources that results from prohibiting merit aid is the more desirable one.

Considering the impact on family incomes, merit award winners will tend to come from affluent families and to have bright future prospects owing to high achievement. No obvious purpose of equity is served by adding to their advantage through a reduced price for college. However, the presence of merit awards might provide an added stimulus to students to perform well in high school, with attendant social benefits. The prospect of merit dollars may induce students to improve their performance both in strictly academic pursuits and in those kinds of extracurricular activities that college admissions committees seem to care about. Under current arrangements, competition to get into highly selective colleges provides a strong incentive to top-ranking high school students but is of little consequence for others. Merit aid at the same class of institutions would probably not change these incentives notably, but to the extent that merit aid extended into the ranks of less selective institutions, it could have a favorable effect on high school students' incentives. We know of no evidence that would help in assessing the size of such effects.

Concerning the impact of colleges' merit competition on colleges' expenditure on other activities, the most obvious place to cut back in order to finance merit scholarships would be need-based financial aid. From both equity and efficiency standpoints, this would seem to be an undesirable trade-off. Schools might, of course, cut back on other types of expenditure to finance merit aid, and some of these might have been wasteful. However, social policies that provide both tax preferences and direct subsidies to higher education indicate that spending by schools is judged on the margin to have net social benefits, so it seems plausible that cutbacks in the activities of colleges, in favor of socially unproductive spending on merit aid, are undesirable.

These are important arguments, and they seem to us to provide good reasons on the whole for discouraging merit competition among institutions of comparable quality. In particular, these arguments may apply with special force to the most prestigious group of institutions, which includes the institutions that were pursued by the Justice Department partly on the ground that agreements not to offer merit scholarships were illegal. Because students already work hard in high school to gain admission to these highly selective institutions, it is unlikely that merit awards would induce any further effort toward good performance in high school. Moreover, the possible beneficial effects of relocating students from more to less selective institutions through merit offers (to be discussed shortly) would not pertain to merit offers from top-ranking institutions. Our judgment is that agreements among top-ranking institutions to eliminate or restrict merit awards are in fact socially desirable.

So far, our analysis has focused only on the aspect of competition that concerns schools with student bodies with similar qualifications. We must now consider the social consequences of the other aspect of merit competition, the use of merit dollars by schools of lesser reputation to "buy" students from more prestigious schools. A key question raised by this issue is the following: What is the socially most desirable way to distribute high-quality students among colleges and universities? Is it better to cluster the most capable students together or to distribute them more widely among institutions, where they will have peers of varying quality?

The existing system of selective admissions (followed by the top schools in the country) is a sorting mechanism in which students with the highest abilities are grouped together, leaving lower-ability students in their own group.[5] What would happen if merit aid had the effect of leading to a more even distribution of students by ability across a range of institutions?

The literature on the effects of alternative groupings of students at the higher education level is rather undeveloped. However, a good deal of work has been done on the "tracking" of students by ability group at the secondary school level. Presumably the gain that is sought in tracking is the greater efficiency of grouping students who can handle similar material and progress at a similar pace. Yet there may be offsetting disadvantages if less capable students learn more in classrooms that include some more capable students. One summary of the literature (Vanfossen, Jones, and Spade 1987) finds that the particular track a student is placed in plays an important role in determining a variety of educational outcomes, including academic performance and educational aspirations.[6]

Why is it that students on a "lower" track end up suffering academically? The authors speculate that teachers may treat these students differently and, in addition, following Coleman et al. (1966), that a critical mass of interested and enthusiastic students is needed to push along the learning process. Another explanation relates to the possibility that some of the best teachers are attracted by the opportunity to teach the best students, and hence teacher quality may vary positively with student quality.

If these findings carry over to college, the educational experience of an average student at an institution that attracts less than stellar students should be less good than the experience the same student would have at an institution where there are a larger number of better students. An alternative allocation scheme would be to group students in a more random fashion—in other words, to increase the amount of mixing of students of different abilities. Taking "better" students away from institutions in which they predominate and putting them in "lower-quality" institutions may improve the educational experiences for all students at these less prestigious institutions if this motivates both teachers and other students to be more engaged in the learning process.[7] Indeed, the pursuit of such an outcome is surely part of the motivation for schools that use merit scholarships to try to recruit some highly capable students to their institution.

But such a scheme would not, using the terminology of an economist, be "Pareto optimal"; that is, there would be some losses to accompany the gains. In other words, the interests of some students would be served along with, quite possibly, the efficiency effects of the higher education system, but some students would be hurt.[8]

An interesting paper by Henderson, Meiszkowski, and Sauvageau (1978) describes these differential effects in detail. Looking at primary school data from Canada, they find that there is a strong peer group effect—that the achievement of individual students depends to a large extent on the quality of their classmates. The efficiency gain from mixing students of different abilities comes from the nonlinearity of this effect: the achievement of individual students rises with an improvement in the average quality of their classmates but the increment in achievement falls as average class quality rises. That is, removing a superior student from a class comprised of other superior students and placing that student in a class of weak students will raise the achievement level of the weak students more than it would reduce the achievement of the class that the student left. Hence mixing weak and strong students raises the overall performance of the student population as the gains of the weak students exceed the losses of the strong students. As the authors point out, this finding is controversial, but it suggests that efficiency gains come at the expense of some students while helping others.

Suppose that it were established that the efficiency of higher education, in terms of the overall achievement level of its students, could be increased by spreading the most talented students more evenly across institutions of higher education. Then merit awards that attract students from more prestigious to less prestigious institutions may work in this desirable direction. If elite colleges that enroll the great majority of highly able students refrain from offering merit awards, other schools may have the opportunity to attract some of these academic stars by offering them attractive financial aid packages.[9] As mentioned, studies suggest that the student may very well pay a price in terms of ultimate educational or financial gain from education. This student is, however, providing educational benefits to classmates, benefits that are, according to the assumption we are making here, greater than those that the same student would provide to others at an elite school. The fact that the student's education is obtained at a lower cost may be seen as appropriate compensation for the benefits to others and tends to offset the possible lower educational returns to the individual students. The advantage of redistributing students in this way, compared to other possible ways of redistributing students among institutions, is that the student relocates voluntarily.

There are obviously serious questions to consider about whether students and their families are able to do a good job of judging trade-offs between such educational benefits and dollars. As more schools have moved aggressively to offer generous merit awards to the very best students, increasing numbers of families will face these difficult dilemmas. Is a Harvard or Princeton or Williams education worth $120,000 *more* than a free ride at a less prestigious institution like George Washington University or Wabash? These questions pose agonizing dilemmas for families, and it is easy to worry that they may make choices that are shortsighted or poorly informed. Yet it is hard to see that anyone else is in a better position than the family members themselves to weigh such difficult choices.

In sum, the social impact of increases in merit aid is not as clear as is usually assumed. Even if merit aid went mainly to students who were already advantaged, if the efficiency increases associated with spreading the most talented students over a wider range of institutions were great enough, less advantaged students might still benefit. If this argument holds, then under certain circumstances there may be equity as well as efficiency gains from expanded merit aid.

However, when merit aid constitutes another reward to students who have already garnered a greatly disproportionate share of the nation's resources and does not lead them to reallocate themselves in a manner that increases total educational output, it is clear that neither our equity nor our efficiency goals would be satisfied. In other words, the best justification from the interests of society would be an efficiency gain associated with a more even allocation of our best students—if merit aid offers from less prestigious institutions succeed in attracting top students who would not otherwise consider enrolling there, efficiency gains might be sufficient to justify this policy from the viewpoint of society. If, instead, merit aid merely redirects a top student from one of our premier institutions to another, it may be in the interest of the individual student, but it is not in the broader interest of society, especially since the opportunity cost of this spending is presumably either reduced support for need-based student aid or some other use of the resources to advance the educational purposes of the institution.

We look next at which institutions give merit aid and then turn to the question of who gets it. We conclude by relating those findings to the theoretical arguments presented here.

11

The Institutional Perspective

NON-NEED-BASED grant aid awarded by institutions in 1983–84 and
1991–92, with the institutions classified by public or private control
and Carnegie classification, is documented in Table 11.1.[1] The sample
is limited to nonprofit bachelors' degree–granting institutions in the
United States. We omitted from consideration institutions that had
missing data in categories of interest for either year. The resulting
sample includes 379 observations. The 1983–84 data are converted to
1991 dollars using the consumer price index. We report non-need
grant dollars (excluding athletic scholarships) per full-time freshman
(including those not receiving aid) for both years, non-need grant dollars as a fraction of all (need and non-need) institutionally funded
grant dollars, and real annual growth rates of non-need and need-
based institutionally funded grants. The final column shows the size
of freshman enrollment in 1992 for each institutional category.[2]

In 1983–84, some 294 of the 379 institutions in the sample (78%)
reported providing non-need-based aid (other than for athletes). In
1991–92, a total of 308 institutions (81%) reported spending on non-
need-based aid.

In the aggregate, it is clear that non-need-based grant aid has
grown quite rapidly over this period. For this sample of institutions
as a whole, non-need aid per enrolled freshman grew from $177 in
1983–84 to $505 in 1991–92 (after adjusting for inflation). The annual
real growth rate was 13%, compared to 10% for need-based institutionally funded aid. Non-need grants in 1991–92 accounted for almost
a quarter of all institutional spending on grant aid. Growth has been
rapid in both public and private institutions. At public institutions,
non-need-based aid accounted for 56% of all institutionally funded
aid in 1991–92, up from 44% in 1983–84. At private institutions,
whereas non-need aid accounted for only 21% of the total in 1991–92
(17% in 1983–84), the dollars per freshman are substantially greater—
$742 at private institutions, compared to $252 at public institutions in
1991–92.

Further insight results from breaking the data down into categories
according to the classification system developed by the Carnegie
Foundation. Institutions are classified into research universities (which

TABLE 11.1
Non-Need Aid per Freshman, by Institution Type and Carnegie Classification, 1983–84 and 1991–92

Carnegie Class	Non-Need Aid per Freshman (in 1991 dollars)		Non-Need Share of All Institution-Based Aid (%)		Real Growth Rate in Aid per Freshman (%)		Freshman Enrollment, 1991–92
	1983–84	1991–92	1983–84	1991–92	Non-Need	Need	1991–92
Public							
Research I	71	296	0.32	0.46	18	11	33,056
Research II	112	525	0.62	0.64	19	19	4,957
Doctorate I	90	185	0.44	0.55	9	2	10,874
Doctorate II	43	108	0.14	0.63	11	−17	1,359
Comprehensive I	101	193	0.51	0.67	8	−1	52,488
Comprehensive II	269	507	0.75	0.63	8	15	4,251
Liberal Arts II	225	852	0.46	0.60	17	10	977
Art and Design	0	0	0.00	0.00	0	−9	1,390
Other Specialized	0	79	0.00	0.67	—	−13	374
All public	96	252	0.44	0.56	12	6	110,003
Private							
Research I	201	474	0.08	0.10	11	8	14,361
Research II	205	1,051	0.10	0.19	20	11	4,757
Doctorate I	46	399	0.08	0.18	27	15	6,322
Doctorate II	379	1,442	0.29	0.44	17	7	2,515
Comprehensive I	328	790	0.32	0.28	11	13	24,808
Comprehensive II	244	768	0.22	0.24	14	12	11,462
Liberal Arts I	203	660	0.10	0.14	15	9	27,156
Liberal Arts II	383	1,040	0.30	0.33	13	11	19,123
Religious	268	618	0.58	0.49	10	11	396
Other Health	266	607	0.39	0.40	10	13	599
Engineering	36	80	0.08	0.08	10	13	447
Business	129	365	0.21	0.14	13	19	3,391
Art and Design	74	513	0.16	0.34	24	11	1,755
Teachers	18	59	0.13	0.12	14	17	170
All private	253	742	0.17	0.21	13	10	117,262
All institutions	177	505	0.21	0.24	13	10	227,265

Note: Carnegie classification as of 1987.
Source: Peterson's Institutional and Financial Aid databases.

receive major funding for supported research), doctorate-granting universities (which receive less external support), comprehensive universities (with graduate programs but fewer doctorates), liberal arts colleges, and various categories of specialized institutions. The first four categories (research universities, doctorate-granting universities, comprehensive universities, and liberal arts colleges) are further sub-classified into two quality levels, designated I and II. In private higher education, the less prestigious research universities (Research II), doctorate granting institutions (Doctorate II), and liberal arts colleges (LA II) have made especially large investments in non-need-based grant aid, with spending per freshman in 1991–92 at $1,051, $1,442, and $1,040, respectively. This can be contrasted with spending at their more prestigious counterparts of only $474 at Research I, $399 at Doctorate I, and $660 at LA I institutions. The two types of comprehensive universities, by contrast, spend similar amounts on non-need-based grant aid.

In terms of changes over time, Research II universities have been investing heavily in non-need-based aid, as evidenced by an annual real growth rate that is almost twice as great as the growth rate in need-based aid (20% versus 11%) and the growth rate in non-need-based aid at Research I institutions (again, 20% versus 11%). Interestingly, while both Doctorate I and Doctorate II schools have also been increasing non-need-based aid far more rapidly than need-based aid (with annual real growth rates of 27% versus 15% at Doctorate I schools and 17% versus 7% at Doctorate II schools), the more prestigious schools in this category have been increasing their non-need-based aid at a much more rapid rate than the others.[3] At comprehensive schools, there is little difference between growth rates in non-need and need-based aid or between institutions of different quality. The same is largely the case at liberal arts colleges, although LA I institutions have increased their non-need-based aid faster than their investment in need-based aid (with annual real growth rates of 15% versus 9%).

Public institutions show many similarities to the trends for the private sector. The research and doctorate-granting universities have targeted a lot of their aid resources on non-need-based grants, sometimes in the face of low growth or decline in overall aid resources.[4] The heaviest investment in terms of dollars per freshman among public institutions occurs at Research II ($525), Comprehensive II ($507), and LA II ($852) institutions. At those schools, the greatest evidence of differential investment in non-need-based aid is at the liberal arts colleges, although the small number of observations makes this finding tentative.

These results suggest that a closer look at non-need-based aid according to the "selectivity" or "prestige" of the institution may be helpful. Table 11.2 examines one selectivity measure, a self-report from the institution on difficulty of entrance, rated on a scale from 1 to 5, with 1 meaning most selective.[5]

TABLE 11.2
Non-Need Aid per Freshman, by Admissions Difficulty, 1983–84 and 1991–92

Entrance Difficulty	Non-Need Aid per Freshman (in 1991 dollars)		Annual Real Growth Rate (%)	Freshmen Enrolled, 1991–92
	1983–84	1991–92		
Public				
2	25	124	20	9,183
3	83	251	14	71,261
4	143	284	9	18,029
5	147	311	9	11,530
All public	96	252	12	110,003
Private				
1	0	1	16	11,683
2	208	640	14	29,547
3	292	924	14	65,322
4	204	665	15	8,486
5	824	899	1	2,291
All private	253	741	13	117,329
All institutions	177	505	13	227,332

Note: Difficulty of entrance is judged by the institution, with 1 as most difficult.
Source: Peterson's Institutional and Financial Aid databases.

For public higher education, there is a clear pattern in the data: the more selective institutions (in 1983–84) had the highest growth rates of non-need-based aid. Public institutions that described entrance as "very difficult" (rated 2) raised their spending per freshman on non-need grants by 20% per year after adjusting for inflation, whereas those rated 4 or 5 ("minimally difficult" or "noncompetitive") raised their spending by only 9% annually. Nonetheless, it was still true in 1991–92 that the largest number of dollars spent per freshman on non-need-based aid was at the least selective among the public institutions ($311), an amount that was two and a half times the level of spending at the most selective public schools ($124).

In private higher education, the most selective institutions represented in this data set reported virtually no spending on non-need awards.[6] The least selective institutions had the highest spending on non-need awards in 1983–84 but increased their spending on non-need-based aid by only 1% annually, while other categories of institutions raised their spending quite rapidly. In 1983–84, the least selective places spent $500 to $600 more per enrolled freshmen on non-need-based aid than other private institutions; by 1991–92, that gap had shrunk to $250 or so, with schools that are "moderately difficult" to enter actually spending more per student than the least prestigious institutions.

The rapid growth in spending on non-need-based aid in general, and academic merit aid specifically (except at the most selective private colleges and universities), is perhaps the most significant finding here. It appears from these data that non-need-based aid is becoming a more important competitive factor for a wide range of institutions.

It is easy to understand why the most selective and prestigious institutions invest less in merit aid than other institutions. These institutions face a substantial excess demand among applicants, rejecting two, three, or more applicants for every one they accept. Given that many of these rejected applicants would be full-pay students if admitted, the opportunity cost of merit awards is quite high: the alternative to a merit student is not an empty bed but rather a student who brings respectable credentials and a substantial tuition payment.

These basic economic considerations have undoubtedly been bolstered by agreement among several groups of prominent institutions to limit their aid awards to need-based aid only, prohibiting non-need merit awards. Although Justice Department actions against admissions overlap practices, which provided a particular mechanism for enforcing these agreements, have led to the abandonment of overlap meetings, Congress passed legislation that explicitly legalized agreements among institutions not to engage in merit aid competition. These agreements are important, but we would also stress that the basic economic incentives for engaging in merit competition are less for highly selective institutions than for others.

A second observation we noted earlier is the rapid increase in the use of merit aid at a wide range of institutions. This upsurge in merit aid, we would suggest, is related to the extended period of demographic decline colleges and universities have endured since the early 1970s. Many institutions are apparently using merit aid as part of a defensive strategy, hoping to preserve enrollment levels and student quality in the face of declining applicant pools. To the extent that this force has been at work, it would be reasonable to expect some abatement in the use of merit aid as demographic trends reverse themselves over the next decade.

Finally, if schools are engaging in either a repositioning or defensive strategy with regard to the use of merit aid, this would imply that merit aid investments are made on a temporary basis. As one index of how much variation there is in institutions' reliance on merit aid, we compared the list of the top forty institutions in use of merit aid per enrolled freshmen in 1984 and 1992. Only eight of the forty institutions appear on the list in both years. This appears to indicate that the commitment to the use of merit aid, at least for schools that invest heavily in it, varies quite substantially over time.

12

The Student Perspective

OUR ANALYSIS of the distribution of merit aid among students draws on the National Postsecondary Student Aid Surveys (NPSAS) for 1987 and 1990.[1] Data were collected for 43,176 students in 1986–87 and for 46,788 students in 1989–90.[2] Included in the NPSAS files are weights that can be used in developing national estimates from this sample.

Tabular Analysis

It is of particular interest to examine merit awards in terms of the race and gender of the students who receive them. These results appear in Tables 12.1 through 12.3. Table 12.1 examines aid distributions over all classes of institutions, and Tables 12.2 and 12.3 consider private and public institutions, respectively. The data reported here focus only on 1989–90. Athletic awards are not included in the awards reported in these tables. Non-need awards both to students who also receive need-based aid and to students who do not receive need-based aid are included in these tables.[3]

Beginning with Table 12.1, we can first note that, aggregating over both institutional type and racial group, a larger fraction of women than men receive awards (8.70% versus 6.95%), and female recipients of awards receive larger awards than male recipients ($1,766 versus $1,578). This pattern of larger and more frequent awards for women than men holds for whites, blacks, and Hispanics, but not for American Indians or Asians.[4] Comparing racial groups, whites are considerably more likely to receive merit aid than Asians, with blacks, Hispanics and American Indians falling in between. Average award amounts for those receiving awards are, however, somewhat smaller for whites than for other racial and ethnic groups. Asians and blacks receive the largest awards on average, with Hispanics and American Indians having average award levels in between.

It is worth noting that a number of different factors may contribute to these results. One consideration is that particular schools may give different awards to otherwise comparable students of different racial or ethnic backgrounds. Students from different groups may also vary

TABLE 12.1
Public and Private Four-Year Institutional Non-Need Awards, 1990

Race	Sex	Students Receiving Merit Aid (%)	Average Merit Award per Recipient ($)	Total Merit Awards* ($)	Sample N	Share of Sample (%)	Share of Merit Aid (%)
American Indian	Total	5.11	1,956	2,785,332	123	0.6	0.4
	Female	3.15	4,137	1,756,257	56	0.3	0.3
	Male	6.96	1,030	1,029,076	67	0.3	0.2
Asian/Pacific Islander	Total	4.53	2,494	28,173,400	1,182	5.1	4.3
	Female	4.01	2,480	11,210,181	526	2.3	1.7
	Male	4.95	2,503	16,963,219	656	2.8	2.6
Black, non-Hispanic	Total	6.53	2,344	60,057,470	1,709	8.0	9.2
	Female	7.60	2,403	42,435,070	1,013	4.7	6.5
	Male	4.98	2,214	17,622,400	696	3.2	2.7
Hispanic	Total	6.15	1,846	25,948,640	1,009	4.6	4.0
	Female	6.46	2,133	16,648,623	543	2.5	2.6
	Male	5.80	1,487	9,300,017	466	2.2	1.4
White, non-Hispanic	Total	8.31	1,601	536,904,687	17,922	81.8	82.1
	Female	9.25	1,671	321,313,568	9,150	42.2	49.1
	Male	7.32	1,507	215,591,118	8,772	39.6	33.0
Total	Total	7.86	1,686	653,869,528	21,945		
	Female	8.70	1,766	393,363,699	11,288	51.9	60.2
	Male	6.95	1,578	260,505,830	10,657	48.1	39.8

Note: Figures reflect non-need awards (excluding athletic awards) at four-year Ph.D.-granting and non-Ph.D.-granting institutions and include grants to students also receiving need awards.

*Calculation based on weights that reflect the relation between the number of students from particular groups in the sample and the numbers in all of U.S. higher education.

Source: National Postsecondary Student Aid Surveys.

TABLE 12.2
Private Four-Year Institutional Non-Need Awards, 1990

Race	Sex	Students Receiving Merit Aid (%)	Average Merit Award per Recipient ($)	Total Merit Awards ($)*	Sample N	Share of Sample (%)	Share of Merit Aid (%)
American	Total	8.48	3,181	2,178,901	65	0.5	0.5
Indian	Female	12.78	4,137	1,756,257	26	0.2	0.4
	Male	5.48	1,623	422,645	39	0.3	0.1
Asian/Pacific	Total	8.04	3,356	21,066,506	704	5.1	4.6
Islander	Female	6.70	3,389	7,778,808	306	2.3	1.7
	Male	9.09	3,337	13,287,698	398	2.9	2.9
Black,	Total	8.91	2,771	27,641,857	872	7.4	6.0
non-Hispanic	Female	9.22	2,966	18,021,964	511	4.3	3.9
	Male	8.47	2,467	9,619,893	361	3.0	2.1
Hispanic	Total	8.66	2,121	11,363,205	519	4.1	2.5
	Female	7.47	2,685	6,867,537	286	2.3	1.5
	Male	10.12	1,606	4,495,668	233	1.8	1.0
White,	Total	16.45	1,911	396,904,314	10,070	82.9	86.4
non-Hispanic	Female	18.59	1,983	238,824,296	5,069	42.6	52.0
	Male	14.19	1,812	158,080,018	5,001	40.4	34.4
Total	Total	15.10	1,997	459,154,783	12,230		
	Female	16.78	2,073	273,248,862	6,198	51.6	59.5
	Male	13.32	1,894	185,905,921	6,032	48.4	40.5

Note: Figures reflect non-need awards (excluding athletic awards) at four-year Ph.D.-granting and non-Ph.D.-granting institutions and include grants to students also receiving need awards.

*Calculation based on weights that reflect the relation between the number of students from particular groups in the sample and the numbers in all of U.S. higher education.

Source: National Postsecondary Student Aid Surveys.

TABLE 12.3
Public Four-Year Institutional Non-Need Awards, 1990

Race	Sex	Students Receiving Merit Aid (%)	Average Merit Award per Recipient ($)	Total Merit Awards ($)*	Sample N	Share of Sample (%)	Share of Merit Aid (%)
American Indian	Total	3.74	821	606,431	58	0.6	0.3
	Female	0.00	0	0	30	0.0	0.0
	Male	7.69	821	606,431	28	0.3	0.3
Asian/Pacific Islander	Total	2.93	1,416	7,106,894	478	5.0	3.7
	Female	2.83	1,542	3,431,373	220	2.3	1.8
	Male	3.00	1,315	3,675,521	258	2.7	1.9
Black, non-Hispanic	Total	5.58	2,072	32,415,613	837	8.2	16.7
	Female	6.96	2,108	24,413,105	502	4.9	12.5
	Male	3.56	1,970	8,002,507	335	3.3	4.1
Hispanic	Total	5.22	1,676	14,585,435	490	4.9	7.5
	Female	6.06	1,864	9,781,086	257	2.5	5.0
	Male	4.31	1,391	4,804,349	233	2.4	2.5
White, non-Hispanic	Total	4.61	1,096	140,000,372	7,852	81.3	71.9
	Female	5.02	1,148	82,489,272	4,081	42.0	42.4
	Male	4.17	1,029	57,511,100	3,771	39.3	29.5
Total	Total	4.63	1,234	194,714,745	9,715		
	Female	5.13	1,321	120,114,837	5,090	52.0	61.7
	Male	4.09	1,115	74,599,909	4,625	48.0	38.3

Note: Figures reflect non-need awards (excluding athletic awards) at four-year Ph.D.-granting and non-Ph.D.-granting institutions and include grants to students also receiving need awards.

*Calculation based on weights that reflect the relation between the number of students from particular groups in the sample and the numbers in all of U.S. higher education.

Source: National Postsecondary Student Aid Surveys.

in the types of schools they are likely to attend (and, as shown, some types of schools give more or larger awards than others) as well as in personal characteristics like SAT scores or high school grades that influence whether schools provide merit aid and how much aid is awarded. The multivariate statistical analysis discussed in this chapter reports results that control for some of these influences.

In turning from the aggregate results to results that compare the public and private sectors, some interesting differences between the sectors emerge. At private institutions, whites are about twice as likely to receive merit scholarships as members of minority groups, while at public institutions, blacks and Hispanics are more likely than whites, Asians, or American Indians to receive merit aid. In both sectors, average awards are higher for minority group members than for whites.[5]

The last two columns of Tables 12.1 through 12.3 provide a useful way to summarize some of the relationships we have considered. These columns show, first, the share of all students who belong to a particular race and gender group and, second, the share of all merit aid dollars devoted to that group. Thus, for example, Table 12.1 shows that women comprise 51.9% of enrollments in all four-year institutions while receiving 60.2% of all merit aid. A similar pattern of allocation of aid dollars by gender is observed in both public and private sectors. The story on distribution of merit aid dollars by race is, however, quite different in the two sectors. At private institutions, 82.9% of students are white, while 86.4% of merit aid dollars are allocated to white students. At public institutions, 81.3% of students are white, but only 71.9% of merit aid dollars are allocated to that group. At public institutions, blacks and Hispanics get a disproportionately large share of merit aid: blacks comprise 8.2% of enrollment while receiving 16.7% of merit aid dollars, and Hispanics comprise 4.9% of enrollment while receiving 7.5% of aid. In private institutions, by contrast, both blacks and Hispanics receive aid shares that are less than their enrollment shares. In both public and private sectors, Asians receive a smaller share of aid dollars than their enrollment share.

Multivariate Statistical Analysis

We can gain further understanding of the determinants of individual merit awards through the use of multivariate statistical techniques, which allow us to examine the influence of variation in a single factor on a student's expected merit award while holding other influences constant.[6]

We discuss first variables measuring academic qualification—the SAT score (or ACT equivalent) for freshmen and the grade-point average (GPA) for upperclassmen.[7] The coefficients on both variables are positive and statistically significant. That is, all else being equal, an increase in the SAT score for a freshman or the GPA for an upperclassman would produce an increase in the expected size of the merit scholarship that the student would receive. Comparing the magnitudes of these two results, we can say that a third of a point on the GPA (for example, a change from B+ to A−) is equivalent in its impact on the expected merit award to a 118-point increase in the SAT score.

We turn next to the effect of several demographic and economic characteristics (gender, family income, and race) on the expected value of the merit award, holding other things constant. Males receive significantly smaller awards than women, after controlling for differences in other characteristics. Students from families with higher incomes receive smaller merit awards. Racial and ethnic differences in expected award levels are not statistically significant, with the exception of Asian upperclassmen, where a negative effect is observed. Turning to institutional categories, attending a public Ph.D.-granting institution or a private institution (regardless of whether it grants doctorates) generally has a positive effect on the expected value of the merit award relative to the value at public institutions that do not grant the Ph.D.

Finally, for upperclassmen, we can compare expected awards for juniors and seniors to those for sophomores. We find no significant difference between awards to sophomores and juniors, while seniors are expected to receive awards that are smaller than those for sophomores. This effect could result either from colleges' treating upperclassmen differently from freshmen or from increases over time in the award levels to successive cohorts of students.

We next separate out private schools and public schools. Beginning with the academic qualification measures, the effects of increases in either SAT score or GPA are virtually identical across the two sectors.[8] Turning to the other explanatory variables, as was found earlier in the aggregate results, freshman males fare poorly, while higher family income is generally associated with less merit aid, although there is no significant link between family income and merit awards for upperclassmen at public schools. As was found in the aggregate results, racial and ethnic differences in expected awards show that Asian upperclassmen attending private schools receive merit awards that are substantially less than similarly qualified white students would receive. In addition, the separate private-public regressions show that a black freshman attending a public institution would expect to receive a merit award that is larger than a white counterpart would.

Differences between institutions that grant the Ph.D. and those that don't depend on the sector in question. A freshman attending a Ph.D.-granting private institution would receive less in merit aid than the same student attending a non-Ph.D.-granting private school. The same is true for upperclassmen. In the public sector, however, there are no statistically significant differences between Ph.D.-granting and non-Ph.D.-granting institutions in the amount of merit aid a freshman would receive. For upperclassmen, attending a Ph.D.-granting public school actually increases the merit award. Finally, comparing juniors and seniors to sophomores, there are no statistically significant differences in merit awards at either private or public schools.

It seems likely that the amount of merit award a student will receive depends not only on the absolute level of the student's qualifications but also on how those compare to the average qualifications of students at the school. Other things being equal, we would expect a given SAT performance to yield a higher merit award at a school where the average SAT was lower.

The aggregate results show that there is no statistically significant difference in the merit award a student would receive for attending a school with an average SAT score below 800 as compared with a school with an average SAT score between 800 and 1000. However, a freshman attending a school with an average SAT score between 1000 and 1200 gets less in merit aid than the same student attending a school with an average SAT score between 800 and 1000. The same student attending a school with an average SAT score greater than 1200 would receive substantially less (more than $8,000 less) than if attending a school with an average SAT score between 800 and 1000. As for freshmen, an upperclassman attending a school with an average SAT score above 1200 gives up a substantial amount of merit aid that would have been received had the student attended a school with an average SAT score between 800 and 1000.

At private schools, the opportunity cost of attending a school with an average SAT score above 1200 (as opposed to a school with an average SAT score between 800 and 1000) is very large, almost $10,000 for freshmen. However, there appears to be no difference in expected merit award level as a function of a school's average SAT at public institutions.

Another way to gain insight into the impact of a student's SAT score relative to the school average is to estimate the increase in merit aid a student can expect for attending a school with an average SAT score below what the student achieved. We created a variable defined as the individual's SAT score minus the institutional average.

Students receive a good deal of merit aid for attending a school with an average SAT score that is low relative to the student's score. In the aggregate, the payment is $12.13 per SAT point: $13.26 per point at private schools and $5.71 per point at public schools. Should a student choose to attend a school with an average SAT score 100 points less than his or her own, these estimates indicate an increase in merit aid of $1,326 at private schools and $571 at public schools.

The regression results provide a consistent picture. As expected, academic qualifications play a major role in the awarding of merit aid. Academic qualifications relative to the average qualifications at a school also play a significant role. Income also matters, with students from high-income backgrounds receiving smaller merit awards, controlling for other student and institutional characteristics, although this factor was more important in 1987 than in 1990, and at private rather than public institutions. Turning to gender, males receive significantly smaller awards than women. Certain statistically significant racial and ethnic differences are also apparent, with Asians suffering in terms of merit aid awards relative to whites, and blacks doing relatively well. Both the Asian and black impacts are stronger in 1990 than in 1987, although it is interesting to note that these racial and ethnic effects disappear when controls for institutional quality are introduced.[9]

13

Conclusion

MERIT AID—GOOD OR BAD?

WHAT DO THE findings outlined in Chapters 10 through 12 imply in terms of the positive and negative impact of merit aid for the nation?

The institutional data show that the less selective institutions in both the public and private sectors are far more involved in merit aid than their more prestigious counterparts. This is encouraging from a social perspective—it suggests that the potential efficiency gains accompanying more mixing of students of different quality may be realized. At the same time, the fact that the most selective institutions are not spending very much to induce top students to attend one high-quality school over another implies that there is little in the way of socially wasteful economic rents. These results should temper any worries coming from our discovery that non-need aid comprises more than half of all institutionally based aid at public schools and about one-fifth of all institutionally based aid at private schools. Nevertheless, the revenue forgone by institutions that engage heavily in merit competition clearly absorbs resources that could otherwise go into the educational enterprise. These costs of merit competition are clearly on the rise.

The final set of regression results described in Chapter 12, which consider the combined impact of the individual student's SAT score and the institution's average SATs, have an especially interesting bearing on the question of whether merit aid has an important mixing effect in U.S. higher education. A student with a given SAT score gains substantially in expected merit award by attending an institution (particularly a private institution) with lower average SAT scores. Or, to put it in slightly different terms, students are generously rewarded for the *difference* between their SAT score and the school's average. Since one school's merit student may be another's average student, this implies that the mixing effect of merit awards is quite widespread.

In sum, it is clear that merit aid works to compensate students for attending schools that are "beneath" them, especially in the private sector. This finding implies that the efficiency gains discussed in

Chapter 10 are a distinct possibility. But what about the equity reper-
cussions? Does a disproportionate amount of merit aid go to students
who already have a variety of advantages? Here the story is more
mixed. Although white students get a proportionate share of merit
aid (excluding athletics) in total, they are overrepresented in the merit
pool at private institutions and underrepresented at public schools.
Blacks and Hispanics have the opposite experience, collecting a disproportionate share of merit aid at public schools while losing out in
the private sector. Asians are underrepresented in terms of merit aid
at both groups of schools. Finally, the evidence that, everything else
being equal, merit aid rewards higher academic qualifications while,
especially in the private sector, providing smaller awards to students
from more affluent backgrounds is encouraging from both an equity
and an efficiency perspective.

Although it is undoubtedly helpful to have a clearer picture of the
role merit aid plays in our higher education system, our understanding of the effects of merit aid is limited by what little we know about
fundamental questions relating to the educational process. If, as expected, merit aid continues to make up a bigger piece of the total aid
pie, it becomes even more important to add to our understanding of
the efficiency and equity effects associated with changes in the distribution of top students. As a former Harvard University director of
admissions argued years ago, "It has not by any means been demonstrated that the overall welfare of the nation or of humanity would
best be served by concentrating all the ablest students in a few of the
strongest universities."[1] The question of the educational impact of alternative ways of distributing students is difficult to research but terribly important to a wide range of concerns about the social impact of
higher education. In addition, we need further study of how merit aid
influences the college selection choices of individual students as well
as of how institutions make decisions about whether and on what
terms to provide such awards. We hope that the basic information
presented here on who gives merit aid, who receives it, and under
which conditions society gains or suffers as a result will set the stage
for additional research into this increasingly important topic.

Part Five

THE FUTURE OF STUDENT AID

14

Where Do We Go from Here?

AN UNDERLYING theme of this volume is that colleges and universities are becoming more strategic in their behavior. Data on the long view of educational financing (presented in Chapter 3) and the more detailed shorter view (in Chapter 7) go a long way toward explaining why institutions are trying harder to identify their objectives and to develop financial aid and admissions plans to help them achieve these objectives. In short, actual and predicted revenue shortfalls—most notably from state operating subsidies on the public side and from sluggish net tuition growth on the private side—have forced schools to become much more clever about a side of their operations that had been relatively neglected.

But this new era of "enrollment management" has significant ramifications for the equity and efficiency of our higher education system, and this development must affect our thinking about national policy. The forces we have examined and the trends we have tracked in this volume suggest that some of the purposes of our higher education system will be met quite well under these changing conditions and that some of the clienteles of our colleges and universities will continue to be very well served. Colleges and universities in both sectors are giving greater attention to good teaching, at least partly in response to greater dependence on tuition revenues and to a sense of a weakened political position. Increased emphasis on merit scholarships in both private and public institutions suggests that opportunities will continue to be very strong for our most accomplished and best-prepared high school graduates. But from the perspective of the nation, we must ask which groups are at greatest risk of not being well served and which purposes of postsecondary education are most likely to be neglected under these changing conditions.

National Policies

Our reading of the evidence is that the group most likely to be placed at risk by the shifting environment of American higher education is the group of low-income students who do not have the strong qualifications needed to qualify for selective private colleges. And the accompanying purpose of the higher education system that is at risk of being shortchanged is that of providing educational opportunity to qualified students of all backgrounds. As we argued in Chapter 5, for increasing numbers of children from low-income families, the only educational choice they can meaningfully consider is the local community college. Although this is a good alternative for many students, the choice of whether to attend a local community college or the flagship state university should not be determined by accident of income and location but instead by aspiration and capacity.

Cutbacks in state funding, which have produced rising public tuitions that have not been offset by increasing aid to needy students, play a large role in this constriction of opportunity. But a growing emphasis on merit aid in both public and private institutions and the increasing use of techniques like "need-aware second review" that restrict the flow of institution-based aid to the neediest students have played a part as well. It is not reasonable to expect that individual colleges and universities, struggling with competitive pressures and funding limits, will find the strength to deal with these trends on their own.

At the same time, the capacity of governments, both state and federal, will be strapped for the foreseeable future by limitations on their ability to raise revenue through taxation. In this environment, we would stress the following considerations as critical to state and federal policies. For the states, it is essential in light of funding limitations that they focus their policies clearly on the fundamental purposes of a public university system. In the relative affluence of the 1960s, it was possible for states to conceive and partly execute ambitious "master plans" that found a place for everyone and provided generous subsidies to all who participated. In an era of greater perceived scarcity, the states should be more disciplined in focusing on the essential public purposes of the state colleges and universities. Foremost among these is that of offering a suitable choice of educational opportunities for students of all economic backgrounds. This purpose, we would argue, should take precedence over the goal of keeping the brightest students in the home state by offering large merit scholarships to high achievers or the goal of offering a deeply subsidized education to all students, including those from families with a substantial ability to pay.

The federal government, never the most important player in higher education from a financial point of view, has seen its role shrink under budgetary stringencies. More than ever, the federal government must seek to maximize its leverage on the higher education system by using its limited resources intelligently. We highlight the following points.

First, the federal government must survey the whole higher education scene and aim to concern itself with matters that are most likely not to be attended to without its help. Most obviously, there is simply no reason from this point of view for the federal government to get into the merit scholarship game, as President Clinton and various members of Congress have proposed doing. If there is one group of students in this country who can be confident of gaining access to a suitable educational option at an affordable price, it is the group of top-performing high school students. The explosion of merit aid through the individual actions of private and public colleges and universities provides significant incentives for many high school students. And if that isn't enough, we must not forget that the system of selective admissions in our nation already provides a powerful incentive for good high school performance. For the federal government to gild that lily is a waste of both energy and resources.

We would lodge this criticism against the president's recently proposed Hope Scholarship Program, the tax credit program discussed in Chapter 8. Eligibility for this tax credit in a student's second college year would depend on earning a B− average in the first year. Although not a terribly high standard, this requirement would cut out a number of hardworking C+ students. The B− standard risks encouraging grade inflation, poses problems of administrative cost and complexity and of potential unfairness across institutions with different grading standards, and will further reduce the prospects for disadvantaged students within the program.[1] It is hard to think of a reason for the requirement except to join the bandwagon supporting some kind of merit scholarship principle.

These reservations apply even more strongly to the president's Honors Scholarship proposal. As discussed in the *Economic Report of the President* (1996): "To focus attention on the value of high school achievement, the Administration has proposed providing $1,000 scholarships to the top 5 percent of every high school class, public and private, for use at college. Although the reward is still based on a relative standard, the goal of these awards will be to make the new realities of the labor market more salient, giving students in school a more immediate reason to strive harder" (p. 206). As we have argued in this volume, there is little substantive need for such a program, since highly ranked high school students have excellent collegiate opportunities. Marshall Smith, undersecretary of education, defends the program on the grounds that its cost (estimated at $132 million per year) is tiny relative to overall federal spending on

grants and loans and that the program has "symbolic" value (Lederman 1996).

But we doubt that this is really the type of symbol the federal government ought to provide. Top-performing students already have
strong incentives to do well. Wouldn't a better symbol be a recommit-
ment to a need-based strategy, reaffirming that every qualified student has a legitimate chance at a good college education? Our judgment is that a consistent program that both actively and symbolically
underscores the continuing importance of educational opportunity for
all Americans is a major federal priority.

More generally, as we have said, we believe that it is high-need
students who do not have distinguished academic records who are
most likely to be neglected in the current higher education climate.
This group is not a powerful constituency in most states, and private
colleges and universities are increasingly reluctant to offer a large discount to a low-income student if they can recruit, say, two more or
less comparable lower-need students for the same cost. The best tool
available to the federal government for promoting the educational opportunities of this high-need group is well-targeted means-tested student aid grants.

The current fashion in policy proposals is to promote educational
opportunity through tax concessions rather than direct expenditures.[2]
Although the rhetorical attraction of this approach is obvious, the expenditures are no less real if they come as tax deductions or credits
than if they come directly. It is much more difficult to target and mon-
itor such tax expenditures than it is to manage direct spending. Moreover, the neediest families are much less likely to wind up benefiting
from tax expenditures like those advocated by the administration
than they are from Pell grants. If the nation embarks on a path of
providing support for higher education through tuition tax credits
and deductions, we see serious trouble ahead.

We argued in Chapter 8 and will discuss further momentarily that
the incentives created by these tax breaks are liable to cause institutions either to raise tuitions or to withdraw support from their own
student aid efforts—both unfortunate by-products of the proposed
plan. Tax benefits, moreover, are of limited value in helping people
who are strapped for cash to pay for college because the relief comes
late, when the tax form is submitted, rather than on the spot, as with
grants and loans. There is also every reason to expect that some pro-
viders of educational services will find ways to help families benefit
from the tax breaks without providing the services the law intends
(see Kane 1997). Although the proposed legislation rules out tax
breaks for "leisure-oriented" instruction, identifying and rooting out

such instruction is a nightmare to contemplate and is bound to provoke outcry from those whose offerings are deemed not to qualify. Congress should remember the lessons learned in bringing the participation of the proprietary schools under control in the guaranteed student loan program before creating a new program open to similar worries.

Perhaps our greatest reservation about tax subsidies for higher education is this: opening up a channel by which revenue can flow through the tax system to subsidize college expenses is like opening up a new, steeper path that a river can follow to the sea. We suspect that tax credits and buybacks, once in the code, would undergo broadening and deepening to allow favored constituencies to benefit more easily. Dollars headed for the tax side will grow over time, and the traditional student aid programs, which are much better vehicles for providing access and choice, will gradually wither.

Our first lesson, then, concerning the federal role in student finance, is that many of the problems the federal government seems eager to address in higher education—help to middle-class families, merit awards for highly able students—are being addressed in other parts of the system. The problem of providing a range of good educational opportunities for high-need students is not being met.

Our second point—one that is just as important as targeting resources to students who need them most—is the need for the federal government to recognize in designing its policies that colleges and universities will react to the incentives those policies create and not passively accept their consequences. We treated this point at length in Chapter 8, emphasizing in particular some of the worrisome incentive effects that might be created by tax credits and deductions for college. There is every reason to expect that both prices and financial aid practices would respond to such incentives in ways that would lead to the colleges themselves capturing a significant fraction of the revenues provided by such deductions. Although, as we have reported in Chapter 8, there is little evidence that increases in federal aid have contributed to the extraordinary run-up in private college tuitions of recent decades, it is in fact likely that tax deductions or credits for college tuition would do just that. This, in our judgment, would not be a good outcome from a national point of view, and surely it is not the outcome envisioned by those who have advanced these proposals. To make this point is not at all to criticize colleges and universities for reacting in this way (if we are right about how they would react). As actors in a competitive system, it is both predictable and reasonable that they would adjust their policies to a changed fiscal environment.

This second point can also be put in positive terms. While avoiding unintended consequences of the incentives it creates, the federal government should also seek when it can to increase the leverage of its programs by taking into account the incentives its programs create. We believe that the program we sketched in Chapter 8, which would provide new supplemental grant funds to students at colleges that met the financial need of their lower-income students, is a good indication of the kinds of possibilities that should be pursued.

Our third point is related to this second one. While being realistic about the forces guiding both states and institutions toward the kinds of behaviors we have examined in this book, the federal government should also seek to identify when those forces push states and institutions toward outcomes that are socially undesirable and should try, within the limits of its powers, to offset those negative effects. Thus, as we have noted, the combination of "need-aware second review" admission policies and the shift toward merit aid, both documented throughout this book, may make a good deal of sense for individual institutions but help explain the worrying trends in college access and choice explored in Chapters 4 and 5. The considerable increases in net tuition for low-income students (detailed in Chapter 3) have led to a growing gap between enrollment rates for high-income and low-income students and to an increased concentration of low-income students at the least costly institutions. With merit aid increasing at a faster rate than need-based aid (Chapter 11), these trends seem likely to be exacerbated in the future.

So how should the federal government respond? The goal should be to keep the focus on need-based aid from eroding, both in direct federal action and in supporting the need-based dimension of state and institutional policies. This stance does not depend on a claim that the merit components of these policies should be forbidden or actively discouraged by the federal government. Our claim, rather, is that the component of policy that needs to be sustained by the federal government is the need-based one. So the federal government should in the first instance actively fulfill its traditional role of providing aid to needy students. It should at the same time create incentives to push individual institutions to promote that goal as well. We have outlined a new supplemental grant program that illustrates this kind of effort.

Increasing funding for the Pell program is the most obvious way to ensure that low-income students will have both access to some type of postsecondary education and some reasonable choice among institutions. Indeed, as we show in Chapter 8, there is some empirical evidence that greater provision of need-based aid by the federal government encourages greater aid expenditures by institutions from their own resources as well. Yet even though gross tuition at the average public four-year school increased by 86% in real terms between 1980 and 1994 (77% at private four-year colleges and 70% at public two-year schools), the real value of the maximum Pell grant fell by 27% over that period.[3] Though President Clinton has consistently called for increases in the maximum Pell grant, there is little hope that the real decline over the past two decades will be reversed anytime soon. Increases in means-tested student aid should receive the highest priority for federal funding in higher education.

Institutional Responsibilities

The men and women who set financial aid policy in our individual colleges and universities are traveling uncharted waters. This book has documented a number of striking changes in the environment and practices of financial aid in U.S. higher education. Rapid changes in higher education pricing and in government support, sustained growth in the use of no-need aid in both public and private colleges and universities, the emergence of student aid as a key instrument in the newly invented business of enrollment management—all these are earthshaking changes for the once quiet precincts of the financial aid office.

From the standpoint of both understanding and recommendation, it is essential to recognize the great differences in the circumstances of different institutions. As Bowen and Breneman argued in their important 1993 paper, for some institutions, student aid is essentially a discount, aimed at enrolling more students and raising net revenues, while for others it is essentially an investment in the composition of the student body. Many schools in the first group lack the means to pursue the policies of "need-blind admission and full-need financing" that often mark the second group. Only confusion and misunderstanding will result from expecting institutions in these very different circumstances to follow the same policies or adhere to the same principles.

We have argued that governments should expect institutions to behave strategically and that in setting their policies, governments should try to take these strategic responses into account. Are there, then, any limits on the policies institutions might legitimately pursue in advancing their interests through student aid? We find it very difficult to articulate hard and fast rules in this area. But there is at least one principle we believe to be of great importance: the principle of honesty and openness in explaining the policies the institution pursues. Such a policy is valuable for several reasons. First, it is essential to allowing students to make reasonable choices among alternatives. If, in fact, applicants will not be admitted from the waiting list if they have applied for financial aid, they need to know that policy to decide whether to withdraw their aid applications. Second, open policies can be discussed and weighed by the community that has a stake in them—trustees, faculty, students, and alumni. Because colleges are not simply businesses but rather institutions held in trust, it is especially important that their policies be capable of surviving examination by their constituencies. Finally, and more abstractly, there is the simple point that certain kinds of practices will never be undertaken if they have to be public. No college would announce a policy of offering less aid to students who showed more interest in the place (as certain kinds of financial aid leveraging policies would do), and no college should have such a policy. With only a few exceptions, colleges and universities are trying conscientiously to find their way through these uncharted waters. Honest public discussion, uncomfortable as it may sometimes be, will in the long run be an aid in their journey.

Conclusion

We began this volume with a discussion of the twin goals of meeting need and rewarding talent that have informed student aid policy from its inception. There is perhaps a temptation to think that the emphasis on need-based aid in American higher education has implied neglect of the goal of rewarding merit. But even apart from the recent upsurge in scholarships explicitly based on merit, it is important to recognize that this is a very one-sided picture of American higher education.

In Chapter 9, we refer briefly to the work of Gordon Winston (1996), who has written persuasively on the fact that the most highly selective schools offer the largest subsidies to all their students, whether or not the students get any scholarship grants. He defines a subsidy as the difference between institutional educational expenditures and the average price the school charges net of student aid. Winston finds that the average subsidy in U.S. higher education in 1991 was around $7,500, with the student paying $3,100 for a $10,600 education. But there is extraordinary variation in the subsidies that schools give. Schools in the highest decile of subsidy providers give an average subsidy of almost $21,000, charging less than $5,000 while spending more than $25,000. In contrast, schools in the bottom decile charge $5,000 and spend $6,500.

Who enrolls at the schools that provide massive educational subsidies? Winston (1996) reports that 38% of students in top-decile schools were in the top 10% of their high school classes, versus only 12% of students enrolled in schools in the bottom decile. And the relationship between institutional subsidy and student quality is even stronger when you break schools down by sector: 45% of students enrolled in private colleges and universities providing the largest subsidies come from the top 10% of their high school classes, compared with 12% in the lowest decile.[4]

The American system of selective admission to a competitive set of institutions tends to sort students with the highest academic qualifications and promise into the institutions with the most ample resources with which to subsidize the students' education. This is the right kind of pattern of resource allocation to wish for in higher education— society surely gains more from investing more in the education of the most talented—although no one really knows how close we are to right in the relative amounts of resources we devote to the education of the more and the less talented.

But it is unmistakable that this is a system that rewards talent in a big way. Indeed, an intriguing irony that we note in Part Four is that merit aid may often work to reduce the disparity in educational resources between more and less talented students. This is because merit awards are often used to attract a student from one of the most highly selective institutions (with the largest subsidies per student) to a somewhat less selective institution where the student's talents will be valued more by the institution.

For the most part, we see the larger forces at work right now in American higher education as forces that will tend to increase the gaps between the "haves" and the "have-nots" among institutions and between the more and the less needy among college students. These forces include a withering of public financial support for higher education and an intensification of the competition among institutions both for students and for the financial support that is available. In this environment, it is of utmost importance that we not lose sight of the role that student financial aid must play in keeping opportunities in American higher education broadly available.

Notes

Chapter 1

1. The history of student aid is discussed at greater length in Chapter 10.

2. Fully 90% of private undergraduate enrollment was at four-year rather than two-year schools.

3. In addition, of course, part of that $11,200 net tuition charge would be financed by loans and work-study jobs for many undergraduates.

4. Revenues are defined as the sum of federal grants and contracts, state and local grants and contracts, state and local appropriations, endowment income, and net tuition revenue.

5. For a more detailed description of these programs, see U.S. Department of Education (1995).

Chapter 2

1. Bowen and Breneman (1993) refer to this type of financial aid as an "educational investment" as opposed to a tuition discount. They suggest that a good way to distinguish between student aid as a price discount versus student aid as an educational investment is to ask whether the provision of student aid increases or decreases the net resources available to the college to spend on other purposes. A tuition discount seeks to do the former, whereas an educational investment does the latter.

2. The number of high school graduates peaked at 3.15 million in 1976–77, fell by 12% to 2.77 million seven years later (in 1983–84), and bottomed out at 2.47 million in 1991–92 (National Center for Education Statistics 1994, tab. 15). It is projected that in the middle of the next decade, the number of high school graduates will just reach 3 million (National Center for Education Statistics 1995b, p. 2).

3. An early statement of the principles behind such self-conscious packaging of aid to meet institutions' goals is found in Ehrenberg and Sherman (1984).

Chapter 3

1. See Chapter 1 for a more detailed description of the various federal aid programs.

2. Though proprietary institutions enrolled fewer than 7% of undergraduate students in 1988, their students received more than a quarter of all Pell grant funds.

Chapter 4

1. Note that the denominator in Table 4.1 is the number of people aged 16 to 24 who graduated from high school within the preceding twelve months,

while the numerator is the subset of that group enrolled in college. The rates in Table 4.1 are substantially higher than the enrollment of all high school graduates aged 16 to 24.

Chapter 5

1. For years, the view that middle-income students—too rich for financial aid but too poor to afford private school tuitions—are increasingly showing up at public institutions has been stated as truth in the national media (see, for example, Kuttner 1989).

2. The selection of the year 1980 was made with the aim of having the income brackets correspond as closely as possible with the inflation-adjusted boundaries.

3. The precise inflation adjusted categories in 1980 would break down as follows: <$10,0000, $10,000–$15,100, $15,100–$30,200, $30,200–$50,200, $50,200–$100,500, and >$100,500. This reflects inflation between 1979 (the 1980 survey asked students to report parents' income in 1979) and 1993 of 99.0%.

4. McPherson and Schapiro (1995) also present data on the distribution of students across income groups at each institutional type.

5. The actual number of first-time, full-time freshmen enrolled at private schools in 1994 was about 395,000.

6. Actual first-time, full-time freshman enrollment at public four-year colleges in 1994 was about 371,000.

7. Actual first-time, full-time freshman enrollment at public two-year colleges in 1994 was about 483,000. Since 1980, community colleges have drawn a larger share of their enrollment from part-time and adult students, which helps account for the decline in numbers of first-time, full-time freshmen.

8. The increased attractiveness of public universities to affluent students is also noteworthy. Their share of upper-income students rose from 26.6% to 27.8%, and their share of the richest students rose from 19.6% to 24.6%.

9. The revenue situation for private four-year colleges (as well as other institutional types) is discussed in detail in Chapter 7.

10. An examination of how different types of institutions have used merit aid in response to enrollment pressures is presented in Chapter 11.

Chapter 6

1. It is important to distinguish the goal of providing access to capital markets for students, by ensuring or guaranteeing loans or by direct federal lending, from the goal of subsidizing interest costs, as by the current practice of having the federal government pay the interest (or forgo collection of interest, in the case of direct lending) while the student is in school. It is desirable for the government to provide all students with access to capital; we argue here that there is no reason to offer middle- or upper-income students interest subsidies beyond those implicit in guaranteeing the loan.

Chapter 7

1. This appeared as Chapter 2 in McPherson, Schapiro, and Winston (1993).

2. For an institution to be included in our data set, we need information on the full set of expenditure and revenue categories for each of the three years. Both the number of schools and their enrollment are presented in each of the tables that follow. There are a total of 694 public institutions in our data set, with a total enrollment in 1994 of 4.1 million students. There are 494 private institutions, enrolling 1.3 million students.

3. The small sample sizes led us to ignore private two-year colleges along with the professional and specialized groups.

4. We have netted out student aid spending because part of this spending is directly "passed through" from federal student aid, and for most institutions the rest is better seen as forgone institutional revenue rather than as spending on educational programs.

5. For the sake of simplicity, we have omitted from our expenditure tables one expenditure category, mandatory and nonmandatory transfers.

6. As explained in the glossary, endowment income is computed by taking 5% of the market value of the endowment at the beginning of the academic year. Endowment figures for many community colleges, public liberal arts colleges, and public comprehensive universities were lacking, and for institutions reporting a figure, it was almost always extremely small. For that reason, ENDOWINC was set to zero for all public schools other than public research universities, thereby substantially increasing sample sizes for those categories.

7. For example, in some states, certain employee benefits (such as pension plans) appear in state government budgets rather than institutional budgets, thereby converting such benefits to off-budget items. The underestimation of public expenditures may be especially important in analyzing capital spending, where significant plant additions may be off budget.

8. Note that instructional expenditures at public research universities have been increasing more slowly than overall net spending, while the opposite is the case for their private counterparts. This finding is for the most part true also for the other institutional classifications examined.

9. Note, however, the very small base on which changes in institutional aid at public institutions are calculated.

10. Mandatory and nonmandatory transfers are ignored so that the seven expenditures items listed in the table sum to 100%.

11. We define total revenues as the sum of our five revenue categories. Unfortunately, our database has very limited data on total gifts (to the endowment and elsewhere). Again, we use a proxy for endowment income to provide an indication of the amount of money that is availed from the endowment.

12. Though our earlier work used a different sample of schools and some different revenue categories, we found that the contribution of net tuition revenue at public colleges and universities rose by 3 to 4 percentage points from 1979 to 1989.

Chapter 8

1. In the late 1970s, the Middle Income Student Assistance Act made federal loans available to all students, without regard to need, on very generous terms. It is plausible that this new source of funding played a role in stimulating the rapid tuition increases that began in private higher education at that time. But the act and the strong incentives it created were short-lived.

2. The data set used in our econometric analyses contained information on individual colleges and universities and was constructed by merging three federally maintained data sets: the Financial Statistics Report from the Higher Education General Information Survey (HEGIS); the Enrollment Survey, also from HEGIS; and supplementary financial aid information from the Fiscal Operations Report and Application to Participate (FISAP). These data were from the academic years 1978–79 and 1985–86. All values were in 1990 dollars and were calculated on a full-time-equivalent basis. Schools were divided into three categories: private four-year colleges and universities, public four-year colleges and universities, and public two-year colleges.

3. For a contrary view see Kane (1997).

4. See Fischer (1990) for an illuminating discussion of how to use federal policy to shape state policy.

Chapter 9

1. An excellent analysis of these strategic dimensions of aid and admissions policy is Scannell (1992), who constructs an example similar to the one presented here.

Chapter 10

1. We are grateful to Phil Wick for permission to draw on his paper throughout this discussion. All quotations attributed to Wick are from this source.

2. Wick reports that the scholarship application requested information about parents' salary, other income, savings, other investments, home value and mortgage, and other indebtedness, among other things. Students were asked to reveal the value of personal property, summer earnings, the willingness of relatives to contribute, and other matters.

3. This section draws on material contained in McPherson and Schapiro (1990).

4. "More ambiguously" because a merit student at a low-ranking institution might be a below-average student at a higher-ranking institution.

5. Cook and Frank (1993) argue that the clustering of top students has increased in recent years.

6. Though there is some degree of consensus on the effect of tracking on a student's future, there remains a great deal of uncertainty regarding the economic payoff to high school quality. Hanushek (1986) reviews this literature. Betts (1995) tests the impact of three measures of high school quality—class

size, teachers' salaries, and teachers' education—on future earnings and fails to find any statistically significant relationships.

7. If resources were allocated in a similar manner—taking some from the "better" schools and giving more to the "worse" schools—the positive effect of this reallocation of students would likely be increased. One study of higher education recommends just such a change. Danière and Mechling (1970), compute expected earnings flows for students with different abilities entering institutions of different quality. When benefit-cost ratios are examined, the conclusion is reached that we have gone too far in an allocation scheme that places high-aptitude students in high-quality institutions and low-aptitude students in lower-quality institutions. The authors recommend that we instead pursue a policy in which additional college places should go to higher-aptitude students who are placed in low-cost institutions. More recent studies on the effect of college quality on future earnings present mixed results. James et al. (1989) find that a student could have a higher economic rate of return by attending a low-cost college, whereas Daniel, Black, and Smith (1995) discover a strong positive impact of college quality (spending per student, faculty-student ratio, college selectivity) on expected income. This finding remains even after controlling for the fact that more talented students typically congregate at higher-quality institutions. Brewer, Eide, and Ehrenberg (1996) find that after controlling for selection effects, not only is there a significant economic return to attending an elite private college or university, but this premium has also increased over time. Behrman et al. (1996) also find a significant economic payoff to college quality. By contrast, Loury and Garman (1993, 1995) recognize the separate effects of institutional quality and of student performance. They conclude that the gain in future income that accompanies attendance at a higher-quality college may be offset by poorer academic performance associated with a more competitive environment.

8. See Brewer, Eide, and Ehrneberg (1996), Daniel, Black, and Smith (1995), and Behrman et al. (1996) for evidence that students could sacrifice future income by attending lower-quality institutions.

9. It is interesting to note that this provides further support for the view that agreements among premier institutions not to award "no-need" scholarships may very well be in the public interest. Such agreements actually make it *easier* for nonparticipants to compete. Emory University, say, can "bid" students away from the Ivies without so much concern about counter-bids if the Ivies adhere to an agreement among themselves not to make no-need awards.

Chapter 11

1. Our analysis of institutional behavior regarding merit aid is based on two data sets maintained by Peterson's: Peterson's Annual Survey of Undergraduate Institutions, a form generally completed by a school's admissions officer, and the Peterson's Financial Aid Supplement, a form completed by the institution's financial aid officer that focuses on financial aid awards to freshmen.

2. Some of the reported categories include a very small fraction of all freshmen.

3. Note, however, that the Doctorate I schools are starting from a much smaller base than the Doctorate II schools.

4. Caution is advised in interpreting the numbers for certain institutional categories due to the small number of freshmen enrolled. For example, enrollment in the public Doctorate II category is only 1,359.

5. Peterson's provides guidelines to institutions for making this rating. For example, institutions ranked "1, most difficult" are those where "more than 75% of freshmen were in the top 10% of their high school class and scored over 1250 on SATs or over 29 on ACT; about 30% of all applicants accepted." Those rated "5, noncompetitive," had "virtually all applicants accepted regardless of high school rank or test scores." The following are the suggested acceptance rates for the other categories: "2, very difficult," 60% or fewer; "3, moderately difficult," 85% or fewer; and "4, minimally difficult," 95% or fewer (but not 100%).

6. Many highly selective institutions were at the time of this survey parties to agreements to confine their student aid spending to need-based awards. It is possible that some non-need-based aid was provided by these institutions in disguised form (for example, by offering to pay for graduate study or by providing guaranteed support for summer research). Other institutions may have declined to report on non-need-based aid, even if they were not party to such agreements.

Chapter 12

1. These are unique among national databases in providing information about family resources and means of financing college that are verified through data obtained from the student, the student's parents, and the institution's records. Similar studies were conducted for the 1986–87 and 1989–90 academic years. In both years, students enrolled in public, private, and proprietary schools (in programs ranging from less than two years to university-level) were sampled.

2. Our analysis is restricted to students attending four-year nonprofit institutions, leading to sample sizes considerably smaller than the total number of students interviewed in the NPSAS.

3. The results described here are largely replicated when non-need awards to needy students are ignored.

4. Note that the representation of American Indians in the sample is very low, which renders any conclusions about this group perilous.

5. The exception is American Indians at public institutions. Note, however, that data for this group are based on just two students in the sample who received merit awards at public institutions.

6. The most familiar such multivariate technique is an ordinary least squares (OLS) regression. However, this technique is inappropriate in the present context because it presupposes that the dependent variable (in our case, the dollar value of the merit award) is normally distributed and ranges

over all possible values. Merit awards, however, are always positive or zero, with many students receiving no merit award. We therefore employ a statistical technique known as TOBIT analysis, which corrects for the presence of a large number of observations with the dependent variable equal to zero.

7. Whenever possible, the analysis described using 1990 data was replicated using 1987 data. Important differences are summarized at the end of this discussion.

8. Note, of course, that substantially lower tuition in the public sector means that an identical merit scholarship constitutes a much higher percentage of total tuition at public schools than at private schools.

9. This last fact does not necessarily imply that racial or ethnic background plays no role in awarding merit aid. For example, if Asians are offered less merit aid than their white counterparts with similar academic qualifications, Asians might then be more likely to attend more selective schools that offer little merit aid to anyone. Thus the fact that, controlling for the academic quality of the institution, being Asian does not appear to affect merit aid awards does not necessarily mean that racial and ethnic differences don't matter. Our analysis is not able to resolve this question either way.

Chapter 13

1. Thresher (1966, pp. 22–23).

Chapter 14

1. See Gladieux and Reischauer (1996) for a similar argument.
2. See McPherson and Schapiro (1996).
3. *Economic Report of the President* (1996, p. 216).
4. SATs provide a similar picture. The mean SAT score at private schools in the highest decile is 1129, compared with 929 for schools in the lowest decile.

Bibliography

Behrman, Jere R., Jill Constantine, Lori Kletzer, Michael S. McPherson, and Morton Owen Schapiro. 1996. "Impact of College Quality Choices on Wages: Are There Differences Among Demographic Groups?" Unpublished paper.

Bennett, William. 1987. "Our Greedy Colleges." *New York Times*, February 18, p. A31.

Betts, Julian R. 1995. "Does School Quality Matter? Evidence from the National Longitudinal Survey of Youth." *Review of Economics and Statistics*, May, pp. 231–250.

Bowen, William G., and David W. Breneman. 1993. "Student Aid: Price Discount or Educational Investment?" *Brookings Review*, Winter, pp. 28–31.

Brademas, John. 1983. "Forward." *Handbook of Student Financial Assistance* (ed. Robert H. Fenske). San Francisco: Jossey-Bass.

Brewer, Dominic J., Eric Eide, and Ronald G. Ehrenberg. 1996. "Does It Pay to Attend an Elite Private College? Cross-Cohort Evidence on the Effects of College Quality on Earnings." Unpublished paper.

Coleman, James S., et al. 1966. *Equality of Educational Opportunity*. Washington, D.C.: U.S. Government Printing Office.

College Board. 1995. *Trends in Student Aid, 1985 to 1995*. Washington, D.C.: College Board.

Cook, Phillip J., and Robert H. Frank. 1993. "The Growing Concentration of Top Students at Elite Institutions." In *Studies of Supply and Demand in Higher Education* (ed. Charles T. Clotfelter and Michael Rothschild). Chicago: University of Chicago Press.

Daniel, Kermit, Dan Black, and Jeffrey Smith. 1995. "College Quality and the Wages of Young Men." Unpublished paper.

Danière, André, and Jerry Mechling. 1970. "Direct Marginal Productivity of College Education in Relation to College Aptitude of Students and Production Costs of Institutions." *Journal of Human Resources*, 5, 51–70.

Economic Report of the President. 1996. Washington, D.C.: U.S. Government Printing Office.

Ehrenberg, Ronald G., and Daniel R. Sherman. 1984. "Optimal Financial Aid Policies for a Selective University." *Journal of Human Resources*, 19, 202–230.

Fischer, Frederick J. 1990. "State Financing of Higher Education: A New Look at an Old Problem." *Change*, January-February, pp. 42–56.

Gladieux, Lawrence E. 1997. "Statement to the Committee on Ways and Means, U.S. House of Representatives." Testimony at the Hearing on Education and Training Tax Provisions of the Administration's Fiscal Year 1998 Budget Proposal, March 5.

Gladieux, Lawrence E., and Robert D. Reischauer. 1996. "Higher Tuition, More Grade Inflation." *Washington Post*, September 4, p. A15.

Hansen, W. Lee. 1983. "Impact of Student Financial Aid on Access." In *The

Crisis in Higher Education (ed. Joseph Froomkin). New York: Academy of Political Science, pp. 84–96.

Hanushek, Eric. 1986. "The Economics of Schooling: Production and Efficiency in Public Schools." *Journal of Economic Literature, 24,* 1141–1177.

Henderson, Vernon, Peter Meiszkowski, and Yvon Sauvageau. 1978. "Peer Group Effects and Educational Production Functions." *Journal of Public Economics, 10,* 97–106.

Huff, Robert. 1975. "No-Need Scholarships: What 859 Colleges Said About Granting Money to Students Without Regard to Financial Need." *College Board Review,* Spring, pp. 13–15.

James, Estelle, Nabeel Alsalam, Joseph Conaty, and Duc-Le To. 1989. "College Quality and Future Earnings: Where Should You Send Your Child to College?" *American Economic Review Papers and Proceedings, 79,* 247–252.

Kane, Thomas J. 1995. "Rising Public College Tuition and College Entry: How Well Do Public Subsidies Promote Access to College?" National Bureau of Economic Research Working Paper No. 5164, July.

———. 1997. "Beyond Tax Relief: Long-Term Challenges in Financing Higher Education." Testimony before the Committee on Ways and Means, U.S. House of Representatives, at the Hearing on Education and Training Tax Provisions of the Administration's Fiscal Year 1998 Budget Proposal, March 5.

Katz, Lawrence F., and Kevin M. Murphy. 1992. "Changes in Relative Wages, 1963–1987: Supply and Demand Factors." *Quarterly Journal of Economics, 107,* 35–78.

Kuttner, Robert. 1989. "The Squeeze on Young Families." *Washington Post,* September 8, p. A23.

Lederman, Douglas. 1996. "Aid for Whom? Clinton Proposes New Merit Scholarships, but Some Question His Priorities." *Chronicle of Higher Education,* February 2, pp. A23, A25.

Loury, Linda Datcher, and David Garman. 1993. "Affirmative Action in Higher Education." *American Economic Review Papers and Proceedings, 83,* 99–103.

———. 1995. "College Selectivity and Earnings." *Journal of Labor Economics, 13,* 289–308.

McPherson, Michael S., and Morton Owen Schapiro. 1990. *Selective Admission and the Public Interest.* New York: College Entrance Examination Board.

———. 1991a. "Does Student Aid Affect College Enrollment? New Evidence on a Persistent Controversy." *American Economic Review, 81,* 309–318.

———. 1991b. *Keeping College Affordable: Government and Educational Opportunity.* Washington, D.C.: Brookings Institution.

———. 1994. "Merit Aid: Students, Institutions, and Society." Consortium for Policy Research in Education Research Report No. 30, August.

———. 1995. "College Choice and Family Income: How Has the Relationship Changed Over Time?" Unpublished paper.

———. 1996. "Tuition Aid We Don't Need." *New York Times,* November 30, p. 19.

McPherson, Michael S., Morton Owen Schapiro, and Gordon C. Winston.

1993. *Paying the Piper: Productivity, Incentives, and Financing in U.S. Higher Education*. Ann Arbor: University of Michigan Press.

National Center for Education Statistics. 1994. *Mini-Digest of Education Statistics, 1994*. Washington, D.C.: U.S. Department of Education.

―――. 1995a. *Digest of Education Statistics, 1995*. Washington, D.C.: U.S. Department of Education.

―――. 1995b. *Pocket Projections: Projections of Education Statistics to 2005*. Washington, D.C.: U.S. Department of Education.

Scannell, James J. 1992. *The Effect of Financial Aid Policies on Admission and Enrollment*. New York: College Entrance Examination Board.

Shea, Christopher. 1996. "Sweetening the Pot for the Best Students." *Chronicle of Higher Education*, May 17, pp. A39–A40.

Stecklow, Steve. 1996. "Expensive Lesson: Colleges Manipulate Financial-Aid Offers, Shortchanging Many." *Wall Street Journal*, April 1, pp. A1, A6.

Thresher, Alden B. 1966. *College Admissions and the Public Interest*. New York: College Entrance Examination Board.

U.S. Bureau of the Census. 1994. *More Education Means Higher Career Earnings*. (Statistical brief.) Washington, D.C.: U.S. Government Printing Office.

U.S. Department of Commerce. 1993. *Statistical Abstract of the United States, 1993*. Washington, D.C.: U.S. Government Printing Office.

U.S. Department of Education. 1995. *Financial Aid from the U.S. Department of Education, 1996–97: The Student Guide*. Washington, D.C.: U.S. Government Printing Office.

Vanfossen, Beth E., James D. Jones, and Joan Z. Spade. 1987. "Curriculum Tracking and Status Maintenance." *Sociology of Education*, April, pp. 104–122.

Wick, Philip G. 1993. "What's Happening with No-Need Scholarships?" Unpublished paper.

Winston, Gordon C. 1996. "The Economic Structure of Higher Education: Subsidies, Customer-Inputs, and Hierarchy." Unpublished paper.

Index

Admissions management:
  ability to pay versus academic promise, 91–94
  admit-deny, 96
  computing ability to pay, differences among institutions, 97–98
  differential packaging, 94, 96, 99
  ethical issues, 100–101, 102–3
  gapping, 96
  merit aid price wars, 98
  need-aware second review, 96–97, 100, 102
  need-blind, full-need approach, 99–100
Admit-deny, 96
Aid-packaging methodology, 7
American Freshman Survey, 43
American Indians, merit aid and, 122–26
Amherst College, 108
Asians, merit aid and, 122–26, 127, 131

Basic Educational Opportunity Grants (1972), 9
Bennett, William, 81, 82
Blacks:
  changing enrollment statistics for, 37–39
  merit aid and, 122–26, 131
Bowdoin College, 108
Bowen, William, 107, 141
Brademas, John, 107
Breneman, David, 141
Brown University, 108
Budget stretch approach to student aid, 16

California, Master Plan (1960) in, 2, 8
Campus-based programs, 12, 27, 83
Choice of college, income levels and:
  brand-name identification, 48
  community colleges, impact on, 48, 49
  comparison by income level and institution type for 1980 and 1994, 43–45
  future of college affordability and, 49–51
  increased student aid and impact on, 47

  for low-income students, 42, 45, 46, 47, 48, 49
  middle-income melt, 46–48
  for middle-income students, 42, 43, 45, 46–48
  private four-year colleges, impact on, 46, 47
  public four-year colleges, impact on, 46
  public two-year colleges, impact on, 46, 47
  for upper-income students, 42, 45–46, 47, 48
Clinton, Bill, 81, 85, 137
College Entrance Examination Board, 6
College Scholarship Service (CSS), origins and role of, 6–7, 9, 109
Community colleges:
  expenditures at, 68, 73
  low-income students and, 48, 49
  revenues at, 68, 73
Comprehensive universities:
  expenditures at, 63–65
  merit aid, 117–18
  revenues at, 63, 66–68

Dartmouth College, 108
Differential packaging, 94, 96, 99
Direct Loan Program, 11, 12

Earnings gaps, 49
Economic Report of the President (1996), 137
Enrollment (See also Admissions management):
  differences for low-income students versus more affluent students, 39–41
  ethnic differences, 37–39
  impact of higher tuitions and lower aid on, 37–41
  labor market advantages and impact on, 40
  statistics and patterns, 10
Equal opportunity issues, 7–8
Ethical issues, admissions and, 100–101, 102–3

Ethnic differences:
    changing enrollment statistics and, 37–39
    merit aid and, 122–26, 127, 131
Expenditures and revenues:
    changes in composition, 68, 73–76
    data set, 55–56
    expenditure categories, 56, 77–79
    expenditures at community colleges, 68, 73
    expenditures at comprehensive univer-
        sities, 63–65
    expenditures at liberal arts colleges, 68, 69–70
    expenditures at research universities, 56–60
    expenditures during 1986 to 1987, 68, 74–77
    expenditures during 1993 to 1994, 68, 74–77
    levels and trends, 56–68
    revenue categories, 56, 79–80
    revenues at community colleges, 68, 73
    revenues at comprehensive univer-
        sities, 63, 66–68
    revenues at liberal arts colleges, 68, 71–72
    revenues at research universities, 60–63
    revenues during 1986 to 1987, 75–76
    revenues during 1993 to 1994, 75–76

Families and tuition costs:
    benefits for the middle class, 36, 86
    decline in families paying, prior to the
        1980s, 25, 27
    increase in families paying, during the
        1980s, 26–27
Federal government aid:
    for all incomes at private institutions,
        35
    before 1975, 27, 28–29
    during 1975 to 1980, 27–30
    during 1980 to 1992, 30
    future of, 136–41
    increasing role of, 9, 11, 13
    for low-income students at public in-
        stitutions, 34–35
    tuition revenue replacing revenue
        from, 25, 26
Federal government aid, tuition increases
    based on amount of:
    campus-based programs and, 83

    current federal policies, 85–90
    differences between private and public
        institutions, 84–85
    income-graded awards, problem with,
        82–83
    Pell grant expansion and, 88–89
    Pell grants and, 82–83
    piggybacked grants and, 89–90
    tax credits or tax deductions, impact
        of, 81, 85–88, 137–39
    theory and evidence, 82–85
Federal Perkins Loan program, 12
Federal research and development bud-
    gets, aid from, 13
Federal Supplemental Educational Op-
    portunity Grant (FSEOG), 12
Federal Work-Study (FWS) program, 12
Financial aid (See Student aid)
Financial aid award letters, problems
    with, 102
Financial aid officers, changing roles for, 18

Gapping, 96
Gender differences, merit aid and, 122–
    26, 127
GI Bill, 2, 6
Grants, 7
    differences between institutional and
        federal/state, 33, 34–35
    Federal Supplemental Educational Op-
        portunity Grant, 12
    Pell, 9, 11, 30, 31, 82–83, 88–89

Hansen, Lee, 39
Harvard College, 107
Henderson, Vernon, 113
Higher education:
    affordability of, future of, 49–51
    cost cutting at, 18
    impact of demographics on, 17
Higher Education Act (1992), 35
Hispanics:
    changing enrollment statistics for, 37–
        39
    merit aid and, 122–26, 131
Honors Scholarship program, 137–38
Hope Scholarship Program, 137
Huff, R., 109

Income levels, college selection and:
    brand-name identification, 48

community colleges, impact on, 48, 49

comparison by income level and institution type for 1980 and 1994, 43–45

future of college affordability and, 49–51

increased student aid and impact on, 47

for low-income students, 42, 45, 46, 47, 48, 49

middle-income melt, 46–48

for middle-income students, 42, 43, 45, 46–48

private four-year colleges, impact on, 46, 47

public four-year colleges, impact on, 46

public two-year colleges, impact on, 46, 47

for upper-income students, 42, 45–46, 47, 48

Institutional grants, aid for low-income students at public institutions, 35

Integrated Postsecondary Education Data System (IPEDS), 55

Johnson, Lyndon, 2

Kane, Tom, 40, 41

Liberal arts colleges:
   expenditures at, 68, 69–70
   merit aid at, 117–18
   revenues at, 68, 71–72

Loans, 7
   Direct Loan Program, 11, 12
   Federal Perkins Loan program, 12
   PLUS program, 12
   Stafford, 11–12

Local government (*See* State and local government aid)

Low-income students:
   aid for, at public institutions, 34–35
   college selection by, 42, 45, 46, 47, 48
   community colleges and, 48, 49
   enrollment differences for, 39–41
   future of, 135–36
   impact of financial squeezes on aid for, 19–20
   institutional grants for, 35
   state and local aid for, 35

Meiszkowski, Peter, 113

Merit aid, 18
   affects on other expenditures, 111

agreements among top-ranking institutions to eliminate/restrict, 111–12, 120

buying of students from more prestigious institutions, 112

distribution of resources based on prohibiting, 111

ethnic differences, 122–26, 127, 131

gender differences, 122–26, 127

growth of, 116, 118, 120

history of, 107–9

multivariate statistical analysis of, 126–29

price wars, 98, 110

quality of education and instructors affected by, 112–14

SAT versus GPA grades and, 127, 128–29, 130

social consequences of, 109–15

by type of institution, 116–20, 123–25, 127–28

within need, 18–19

Middle-income melt, 46–48

Middle-income students:
   college selection by, 42, 43, 45, 46–48
   tax credits and tax deductions, benefits of, 86

National policies, role of, 135–41

National Postsecondary Student Aid Surveys (NPSAS), 31, 122

Need-aware second review, 96–97, 100, 102, 136

Need-blind, full-need approach to student aid, 8, 16, 17
   admissions and, 99–100

Needs analysis system, 2

Nixon, Richard, 2, 30

Non-need-based aid (*See* Merit aid)

Pell grants, 9, 11, 30
   changes in targeting of, 30, 31
   expansion of, and impact on tuition, 88–89
   problems with, 82–83

PLUS program, 12

Princeton University, 107

Private institutions:
   financial aid differences at, 10–11
   financing of undergraduate tuitions in for-profit, 32, 35–36

Private institutions (*cont.*):
  financing of undergraduate tuitions in
    nonprofit, 32, 33
  future of, 50–51
  income levels and selection of, 46, 47
  key forces influencing, 19, 20–21
  merit aid at, 117–18, 119–20
  sources of revenue for, changes in, 25,
    26
  student aid as a management tool at,
    15–16
Public institutions:
  financial aid differences at, 10–11
  financing of undergraduate tuitions in,
    32, 33–35
  income levels and selection of public
    four-year colleges, 46
  income levels and selection of public
    two-year colleges, 46, 47
  key forces influencing, 19–20
  merit aid at, 117–18, 119
  sources of revenue for, changes in, 25,
    26
  state financial squeezes and impact on,
    19
  student aid as a management tool at,
    16

Research institutions:
  expenditures at, 56–60
  future of, 51
  merit aid at, 117–18
  revenues at, 60–63
Revenues (*See* Expenditures and revenues)
Revenue sources, changes in:
  changes to families, 25–26
  decline in federal research support, 27
  decline in state and local government
    funding, 27

SATs (Scholastic Aptitude Tests) versus
  GPA grades, merit aid and, 127,
  128–29, 130
Sauvageau, Yvon, 113
Shea, Christopher, 101
Smith, Marshall, 137
Stafford loans, 11–12
Stanford University, 109
State and local government aid, 13
  decline in, 27, 50
  future of, 136

impact of financial squeezes on low-
  income student aid, 19–20
impact on state universities, 50
for low-income students at public institutions, 35
tuition revenue replacing, 25, 26
State universities, future of, 50
Stecklow, Steve, 101
Strategic maximization approach to student aid, 16–18
Student aid (*See also* Merit aid):
  budget stretch approach, 16
  evolution of, 5–9
  future of, 135–43
  impact of demographics on, 17
  impact of lower, on enrollment, 37–41
  impact on the development of higher
    education, 9–13
  institutional responsibilities, 141–42
  as a management tool, 15–16
  national policies, 135–41
  need-blind, full-need approach, 8, 16, 17
  need versus merit, 5–6
  1992 legislation, impact of, 35–36
  statistics and patterns, 10
  strategic maximization approach, 16–18
Student aid, sources of:
  campus-based programs, 12
  federal aid before 1975, 27, 28–29
  federal aid from 1975 to 1980, 27–30
  federal aid from 1980 to 1992, 30
  increase in institutional grants from
    1980 to 1995, 30
  Pell grants, 9, 11, 30, 31
  Stafford loans, 11–12

Tax credits or tax deductions, for tuition,
  81, 85–88, 137–39
Tuition:
  decline in families paying, prior to the
    1980s, 25, 27
  decline in state/local government
    funding and affects on, 27
  financing of undergraduate tuitions in
    private for-profit institutions, 32, 35–36
  financing of undergraduate tuitions in
    private nonprofit institutions, 32, 33
  financing of undergraduate tuitions in
    public institutions, 32, 33–35
  impact of rising, on choice of college,
    42–48

impact of rising, on enrollment, 37–41

increase in families paying, during the 1980s, 26–27

increases caused by increased federal aid, 81, 83–90

Pell grant expansion and impact on, 88–89

as revenue, replacing government spending, 25, 26

tax credits or tax deductions for, 81, 85–88, 137–39

University of Vermont, 108

Upper-income students, college selection by, 42, 45–46, 47, 48

Wellstone, Paul, 88
Wesleyan College, 108
Whites:
    changing enrollment statistics for, 37–39
    merit aid and, 122–26, 131
Wick, Philip G., 107, 108, 109
Williams College, 107, 108–9
Winston, Gordon, 142, 143
Work programs, 7
    Federal Work-Study (FWS) program, 12